Broken Vision

Horacio Jones

Orders by U.S. at www.HoracioJones.net

For details, contact the author at the web address above.

Printed in the United States of America.

All rights reserved.

ISBN: 978-1503126268

ISBN-10: 1503126269

This information presented herein represents the view of the author as of the date of publication. Due to the rate at which conditions change, the author reserves the right to alter and update his opinion based on new conditions. This material is general dating advice only and is not intended to be a substitute for professional medical or psychological advice. This book contains profanity not suitable for children.

DEDICATION

Dear Mother,
I want to thank you for always believing in me, supporting me, and helping me embrace the things that I think and feel as strengths, and not weaknesses.

Dear Dad,
I want to thank you for being in my life. Without you, I do not know what kind of man I would have become.

To the both of you,
You're always there to help me in any way with all of the loving things you've done for me. I may never be able to repay you. I've learned what to do and what not to do by observing your 40 year relationship and marriage. Thank you.

Love Always, Your Son,
Derrick Jones, Jr

"I CAN ONLY SAVE MYSELF"

Table of Contents

I Am Not A Love Doctor

ACKNOWLEDGMENTS

Thank you to the following individuals who, without their contributions and support, this book would not have been written:

Sylvester McNutt III
Britney Sade

Forward:

Sincerity seeps through the words of a once broken man while understanding he is assigned to the vision of a leader. So here we have Broken Vision; where those noble worlds unite with the courtesy of Horacio Jones. Mr. Jones fondles the essence of our indecisiveness by confronting every lovers concern head on. It is his seamless permutation of tone and truth which resonates with me, and provides the clarity for that which had become so out of focus. It is his transparency which breaks down the walls of stubbornness and greets our emotions with the language of brotherly love. It is his vision of how love can be, which ignites the flame of hope. You can dare to be a man who tackles truths as he does. You can dare to be a woman who appreciates him. But, you won't dare to stop flipping the pages of this masterpiece, as he sweeps through the thoughts you doubted that anyone else knew existed. Hereto is your confirmation.

The Broken Vision is more than the state of being broken, because it is also the revelation of a lesson – it is transitional. This Broken Vision is where the signs become so crystal clear and the destination nears. You may have never noticed how long you were aimlessly wandering in a Situationship but, I know you can still remember that moment when your heart was broken and you knew then more than ever, you would have to make the hardest decision that **needed** to be made.

The Broken Vision is where you collect your pieces so you may find peace. Horacio reveals the ugly truths and smothers the ache of the disappointment with an abundance of delectable food for thought (some are an acquired taste). The moment we accept these feelings of disparity as lessons, we become victors of life. Marinate on that for a moment … This can single handedly liberate you from the denial and prepare you for a better love – the love that you desire.

If you find yourself questioning the purpose of the heartache that finds you, look at the way you allow people to love you. This vision does not exclude self-accountability. More often than not, truths expose just as much about ourselves because we are responsible for what we tolerate and how we react. Move from the cloud of defensiveness and be receptive to the idea that you enabled bad behavior by being faithful to it.

We all have habits of romanticizing the time in an effort to negate the inconsistent love. Most of us fall into the safety net of familiarity in fear that the freedom of real love does not exist. This is self-entrapment; love is emancipating. Horacio surrenders his own experiences as a reminder of our common ground then proceeds to release us to where we hope to be. The discomfort that you may feel is the process of being removed from your comfort zone, so that you may experience the newness that you were blocking all along.

Growing pains are the bittersweet luxury of adulthood. We are finally free to be the person that adolescence may have been too shy to reveal. We are finally liberated into the possibility of self-acceptance in entirety. The love that you seek cannot be defined by anything other than finding someone who wishes to live eternally in your space of freedom. With that said, love shared with your soul mate, will not hurt from the restrictions they wish to place upon you. It will promote your growth as you continue to grow into newfound territory with them. Horacio links the heartache to the healing, and the healing to the completion. The completion is not merely partnership; it is self-love to the utmost degree.

So indeed, that which is broken can be fixed. Contrary to our discouraging feelings however, the resolution is self-fulfilled. This is the declaration of the intention of your journey in love – to learn. In your very hands is this conscious piece of literature from a man who did not allow his brokenness to render him unrepairable and keep him that way forever. Horacio continues to grow, like us all.

In this work, Horacio Jones reassembles the shattered pieces of himself, takes a step back – like a Kintsugi exhibit at the museum – and reflects on how each fracture is a bridge to the next chapter. We find our wholeness at the core of this... Broken Vision.
Britney Sade
Moments of Transparency
North Babylon, NY

Horaciology

My mission is not to save anyone other than myself. I cannot help people. I can only grow as much as I can for myself and use my gift to help others seek growth by showing them mine. I am not a relationship guru. I am not a relationship doctor. I am only an observer of relationships, and a seeker of true love. With that being said, the words in this book are what I truly believe within my heart. I do not claim to have the answers, I only have my perspectives, opinions, and frustrating contradictions. I am not right, nor am I wrong. I just "am."

If you bought this book, it is because we relate in many forms, and you want to appreciate it from another perspective. In addition, you do not **need** advice, you **want** something, or someone, to show you that you are not alone in what you feel. Please understand that when I say "you", I am always speaking to myself first.

Broken

Sometimes, we attempt to explain what love and happiness is. No matter which definitions we give, they are always different. Love makes no sense. I will not try to make this book into something that it is not. Honestly, I am writing this book because I need to exhibit my point of view. I need to let go of the thoughts that I usually drag along in the back of my mind. They have become so abundant, that I cannot seem to let them out on one sheet of paper, or one Instagram post. It is as if the pages of my journals are too fragile for the weight of my words.

Vision

My vision is to move people, inspire new thoughts, and contour new perceptions about relationships. When you are autonomous by your imagination, the ideas that you explore and discover are a lot more appreciated and interesting. That is why I have an irresistible passion that I certainly cannot contain. What I like best of all is the beauty of the concept: creating an amazing idea from my mind, and conveying it to another's. It is beautiful beyond description because it is going to HELP people get through tough situations.

Mended

Although, I've been hurt by my past relationships, I have not given up on love. My philosophy has always been to love as much as I can no matter how much I've been hurt and betrayed. Even when a relationship does not work out, I'll always be able to accept the outcome by reminding myself that I gave it my all, and that my effort was not the issue.

Sight

It is said that we should never ask a single person for relationship advice. I disagree. Every "single" person is not trying to ruin relationships; not all misery wants company. If you think that they do, it is like saying that all single people are lonely and miserable. Loving you and giving yourself time to heal, and not settling for just anyone has never caused anyone harm.

So, YOU need to reevaluate YOUR relationship if you find yourself asking ANYONE, single or not, for advice. Just because they are in a relationship does not mean that they will give you good advice. Just because they are not in a relationship does not mean they will give you bad advice. At the end of the day, it is YOUR heart on the line. However, other perspectives can help.

You Bought My Book That Makes Us Family.

If you want to do some soul searching, or to hear something you already know, but needed confirmation that you weren't going crazy, then this book is for you. Broken Vision consists of my observations, experiences, clarity, and reality. I believe that no matter who you are or what background you have, there is something in this book that will resonate with you and leave you "thirsty" to read more.

Situationship

Some of us want to have a commitment in place before we take a big leap into a relationship activities. However, confusion arises when one of us does not want the commitment and only wants the benefits of a relationship. Most people think that the confusion and uncertainty in this generation's form of dating is a complete two-way street. I'm sorry, it is usually not. In most cases, they already know what the hell they want. In their minds, they have made it clear that they do NOT want a relationship. But, we go along with it and our compliance shows that we are okay with it. Nevertheless, they are cool with doing "relationship-like" things because in their mind, they ALREADY made it clear. We, on the other hand, are left confused, hoping for more by:

1. Continuing to offer more attention, hoping it will change their mind. "Proving our worth"
2. Pretending to be perfectly ok with just being friends with benefits until further notice.
3. Overly expressing our willingness to wait until the other person is "ready".
   4. Falling for their potential.
   5. Trying to convince them that we were perfect together.
6. Trying to force ourselves to love this person and manipulate them into falling in love.
7. having sex with them. (Miraculous sex is often what keeps the perplexing nature of a Situationship going. Besides being the sporadic cure for loneliness, sex is the key facilitator of this dysfunctional style of dating. No one wants to be horny and lonely).

A ***Situationship*** is an entertaining, but complicated in-between phase of being more than friends with benefits. It is an arrangement that deems you to be less than official relationship partners without a label, where two people haven't committed to being anything official for who knows what reasons. Are you two together or NAH?

Situationships: - having sex, thinking that it is official when it is actually unofficial, having a bond without a title, having the title without a bond, not being ready for a relationship, but ready to ACT like it is a relationship, messing around with someone for months or years who can only "see you in their future", while giving excuses for why they won't settle down with you, NOT committed, - situation "ships" that sink.

*** This includes you and your ex who you still mess around with when you are broken up. The interesting thing is that more often than not, it never turns (back into) into an official relationship. Why? **Because we allow people to treat us like they own us, without giving us a title or commitment.** We allow them to get used to that arrangement. As a result, they see no point in "leveling up" to an official relationship.

We are not together

Why aren't you REALLY together???

They want the company, security, sex, and attention but they do not want the EMOTIONAL RESPONSIBILITY of being your partner.

Let me guess, they like things **"the way they are"**. This is usually because they know that if things go well, you, your friends and family and their friends and family will start having expectations of marriage and kids in the future.

It is difficult for you to understand why someone who is clearly enjoying the "**bonding**" with you would not WANT it to progress to something long term, but that's the way some of us are; we love the benefits, not having to commit to them.

"So why are they messing with me?"

It's not that they are afraid to commit to the you… it's that they REALLY aren't that into you… but into you enough to have your companionship, emotional support, and sex. The friends with benefits Situationship suits their lifestyle, for now. They like you. They enjoy your company and sex. They enjoy how you make them feel and they are having fun just **"going with the flow."**

Then why are they making such an effort to help me out when I need it and why introduce me to family?

They enjoy supporting you when you really need them because it allows them to play the "**giving woman" or "protective guy**" role for a while and makes them feel good about themselves, but they ARE ONLY PUTTING ON A SHOW. They do not want to be your giver/protector FOR REAL and not forever.

They introduce you to family and friends because they feel comfortable enough to do it. Think about it, all of their other friends meet the family. Why can't you? Because you're having sex?

"We are not together" because of "**expectations**" and no one wants an embarrassing public break up. We don't want other people to know our "business".

However, people who really want a future together would be willing to tell anyone. Someone that really wants you will give you that label or confirmation of your relationship status. Not **"we do not need a label because it complicates things."** Yeah, of course it is complicated as hell now that your side pieces know about your relationship. It is complicated because you are still entertaining other people. That label is a way of letting everyone know that you are proud of being with someone, and that you have long term plans with them. The label, actions and discussion goes hand in hand to stop the bond from being complicated. When everyone knows your relationship status, your secret life becomes "complicated."

Situationships are Fake-Relationships

Situationships are superficial. Situationships have all of the benefits of a relationship without the label/commitment. They seem to be laid-back substitutions for relationships because you get the relationship benefits, but you also get to maintain your "**singleness**." Believing that you get the **"best" of both worlds** is exactly why **Situationships** get complicated.

It is confusing for some people when one minute you claim that you do not want a relationship, and the next minute you act like you are in a full blown relationship. You spend time, have sex, meet friends and family, and do not want each other to talk to other people. You put all of that time and effort in for what? Just to say you are not in a real relationship? Then turn around acting single as hell all over again... On top of that, you don't mention what you REALLY want because you do not want to lose the halfway-relationship.

Why should they want the labels if we are ALREADY giving them everything that a commitment represents? They are able to get whatever they want, and when it comes time to reciprocate, they use the "we are not together" excuse. What we do not understand is that our actions are of an official relationship partner, but our commitment and label is NOT official.

The Place Holder

Have you ever messed around with someone for months and months but they said they didn't want anything serious with you? But they met someone else and all of a sudden they wanted a relationship with **them?**

So you thought, "It was supposed to be me".

How did it happen? You want to know. "Why them – and not me?"

Well, because you were the place holder. You were just a placeholder, a temporary convenient "chill" partner until the woman or man they REALLY wanted came along. You were ok with faking a relationship with someone and then they ditched you for someone else. You don't know what the hell you did wrong. You don't know what made them choose the other person over you after all of that time; they basically just left you hanging. Why?

This is difficult to explain because they may truly believe that they do not want ANYONE. Not you, or a new person. Suddenly, they change their decisions about relationships when the NEW **"the one"** comes along. While it is a shock to them, it is also a shock to you (the placeholder), unfortunately.

This may hurt: The NEW **"The One"** rarely has to **"try"** to be the one. they just **"ARE"**, and I know it does not make any sense to YOU, because that other person may not even come close to you in comparison with most desired qualities for a relationship partner. Nevertheless, the **COMMITMENT "spark"** with you just isn't there. It's not because you are not good enough, it's because they just don't feel that desire to be committed to you like they do to the new person. You have to try to spark things up; that other person just exists and we automatically feel something for them, not you. This does not mean you are less of a woman/man. It just means that we do not feel the same spark with you, as we do with the other person. That's life.

The issue is when we don't tell you sooner that we don't want more with you, then leave you hanging. A lot of times, we stick around because we like you and we love the benefits we get while messing around with you. A lot of times, we stick around because we like you and we love the benefits we get while messing around with you. Then all of a sudden, this new person comes along and we start feeling something for **them**. Now we want a relationship, **with them**. So, you're like, "**but I thought you didn't want a relationship**?" We didn't... with YOU. It just took a while to realize it. It just took meeting someone new to realize it. Not only that, there is something about THEM that we can never explain.

Having sex with you, and practicing a relationship with you is only temporary (we are not timing it, we are just chilling, and going with the flow). We are not aware of **"the one".** We just know that YOU ARE NOT THEM; you are holding their place, and when they come out of nowhere, we ditch the placeholder (you) who was playing the girlfriend/boyfriend role: cooking, cleaning, sex, sex, sex, providing snacks, loyalty etc. just to settle with the person we actually want more with.

A lot of times, we stick around because we like you and we love the benefits we get while messing around with you. then all of a sudden, this new person comes along and we start feeling something for them. Now we want a relationship, with them.

How do you know if you are the place holder?

You are a placeholder when you are obsessively proving your worth to someone and you are making it blatantly clear that you are a suitable relationship candidate, but they keep stringing you along... and you stay. This goes on for months and years. They come up with millions of reasons for why they can't give you the commitment because you are holding the place of someone else. They may not know who that someone else is, but you are **currently holding the place of a relationship partner without being the official relationship partner. You are a placeholder.**

What makes them commit?

Someone who gives them enough time and space as they need to be THEMSELVES and not have to feel pressured into giving more. On top of that, they commit when they FEEL like it and when they CHOOSE to. This does not mean that you should pretend (or lie to yourself) to want time and space away from each other and it definitely doesn't mean to pretend you're someone else just so they can commit to you. It means that you are not compatible. It means that they do not want the real you.

Will they commit if you hold your place down long enough, proving your worth?

In most cases, hell no. I am pretty sure you have found out that just because you are a suitable partner, people STILL won't choose you if they just don't have the desire too. But, if they get lonely enough and meet someone who doesn't need anything more than what they are comfortable giving, they might settle for a little while.

But don't let that temporary relationship be with YOU!

There's a reason these **"I don't want a relationship"** types end up falling for someone other than us. It's because we weren't on the same page. We both know it. We just have to accept it and replace EACH OTHER.

I Do Not Know What I Want

Let's say you have been fooling around with someone for a while and then you start wondering what do they want from you. Maybe you already know what you want and you just want to see if they are on the same page. The problem is that we are STILL messing around with someone who CLAIMS that they do not know what they want, but at the same time, they know what they do not want for sure: **a relationship with place holders**. They *know* what they want. However, it is difficult to explain and express it in words. Even their actions may confuse you.

They don't want you in the way that you want to be wanted.

They don't want you, and they don't want anyone else to have you. They might not really know who else that they want to be with, but they know for sure that they do not want to be with you.

They *really* don't know what they want.

The last time I checked, it was okay to be confused. But if the person you're dating really doesn't know what he or she wants, they aren't pleased about even talking about relationships. The best thing to do in that case is to give the person's space and if they really want you, they will find you and let you know. Most times, they won't go looking for you in the way you want though.

I don't want to hurt your feelings.

Sometimes "I don't know what I want" is "I don't want to hurt your feelings" said nicely.

I just want to slow down and go with the flow.

Maybe you feel that it's time to finally decide the direction of the bond. Are you going to be together committed, or are you going to let things go? But the person doesn't feel ready to make any.

I'm too damaged.

If the person you've been dating for a while uses "I am too damaged," this is a big ass red flag of emotional unavailability.

In almost all cases, when you hear, "I don't know what I want, I'm too damaged" give the person space. Sometimes this means ending the relationship and letting the person figure out what they do want without hurting you in the process.

17

I really don't know what I want.

Sometimes people are confused. This
means they most likely need time and
space to deal with their confusion so that
it doesn't confuse you. If they decide you
are what they want, they probably know
how to find you.

A word of caution though. If a person sets
a pattern of not calling, not scheduling
dates, and not progressing towards a
relationship with you after several
months, you may want to re-assess if this
is the right person for you

Loyal Booty Call

Dear A1 Booty Calls: They know that sex with you is **basically guaranteed** even though they don't have to actually date you. They just have to send a quick text, and you bring quick sex. Then you leave... knowing damn well you wanted more than sex from them. But you accept the regular hookup with no real outside-the-bedroom interaction/ relationship as a booty call because you hope it would progress to more someday.

You probably ignored the thousands of times that they told you that they didn't want anything serious. You probably ignore how that person sees you. When someone is excited about you, they are going to flaunt you like you are a trophy. They are going to feel great around you and let you know with no doubt. They are going to want the world to see you! They will look at you as an award in a lot of ways, and want everybody to see what a beautiful amazing person they have on their arm.

Do you feel like this person Is promoting you at all? NO? then, yes, you are the loyal booty call because you choose to stick around.

How to know If you are a booty call?

Well, first of all, There's no statistics out there stating if you sleep with someone on the 2nd date, it leads to a booty call roles. Therefore, one of the only ways to figure out whether or not you are a booty call is through experience and interaction with the person. When you are a booty call, the interaction with you will always be limited. There will always be an excuse for why they can't spend more time with you or be seen in public with you and they will usually do this by providing a distraction to avoid constant communication with you. You never get the chance to meet the family and friends. This is probably the biggest red flag **because people who want you will show you off to the people that are important to them.** Most of the time is spent texting or having sex . They never show you off to friends that are of the opposite sex. They never talk about the future and plans for a relationship. In fact, any time you bring it up, they make you feel bad for doing it. They text you at random times asking what are you doing or are you up. They

aren't really concerned about your well-being, they just want to see
if you're up for it sex tonight.

Having sex on the
Regular but are not
Really a couple.

You stop going **OUT**
to places after you've
both gotten intimate...

Do they text or call you
consistently to talk
about meaningful things
or just wants you to "come
through?"

Are they optimistic about the
future and is enjoying getting
to know you more by SHOWING
you with their actions or just
their words?

Know what you getting yourself
Into. Ask questions. Make up your
Own mind or else they will having
Settling for only what they want.

How to Avoid the Loyal Booty Call Role:

1. I'll resist falling for potential.
2. I'll seek a commitment before intimacy. Did I have sex with them just because I like them and got horny as hell, or because they "earned" it? Do I expect a relationship just because I had sex with them? Do I expect them to drop their other options?
3. I won't go with the flow forever, instead, I will communicate what I really feel and what I really want.
4. I'll increase my effort when I trust them.
5. *"I do not want a relationship"* means *"I do not want a relationship with you"*. It doesn't automatically mean they want a relationship with someone else, but it definitely means that they do not want a relationship with me. Being clear from the jump as to what I am looking for before investing feelings and energy is key.

I think the key is defining what Loyalty means to you. Are you really being loyal to someone who doesn't want anything more with you other than convenience sex and chill? If so, you are enabling them, not being loyal. By enabling, you are creating an atmosphere in which they can continue their unacceptable behavior. In other words, if you let them treat you like a booty call, you can't be surprised if they continue to treat you like a booty call. You are allowing it.

I think people don't realize that you will develop feelings for someone when spending a lot of time with them... especially if you're having sex even when the time basically consists of late nights and early mornings sex and nothing else.

Feelings are fine, and getting hurt is part of life (because if you didn't then you wouldn't be trying) but you have to ask yourself if it is still worth it to allow someone to string you along?

HORACIO JONES

What Are We?

We all know what it feels like to have the *"What are we"* question running through our anxious brains all day. If you're in that awkward *more-than-friends-but-less-than-a relationship* stage and have not yet established any sort of relationship, you're only human if you find yourself worrying, wondering, and hinting about it until they too can no longer take it.

Spending more time together is a sign of progress. Eventually, we want to know where the bond is progressing to. After a while of hanging out and being intimate, we tend to fall into this "idk" situation. Seeking clarity and an update on the state of the relationship, we ask, *"what is this, what are we?"* But they respond with something like "Going with the flow, it is what it is". I mean, who actually knows what that means? *"Going with the flow"* and giving a million other excuses is how they take advantage of our confusion. "Going with the flow" REALLY means that they don't want to get serious and probably do not want to even start talking about it.

The way we speak and the time during which we ask, "What are we?" are the factors that need to be considered, because let's be honest, the majority of us have not been blessed with the courage to be so blunt. We either think that we will push them away or we think that we waited too long to ask.

Yo, be blunt as hell when it comes to things that are important to you. I'm not really a fan of being "indirect" or "beating around the bush" or waiting for someone else to make a decision before I let them know what I want when I already know what I want with them. In fact, I absolutely hate it waiting to admit what I want. So, I tell them what I want with them before asking *"where is this going."*

In my opinion the number #1 reason why people end up being strung alone in the "what are we" stage is due to their inability to be upfront and express their true desires in a confident manner and state their interests and intentions in an truthful, straightforward manner. That is in my opinion why the majority of people continue to settle with not knowing what they really are to someone.

You haven't applied that pressure on that ass. You are afraid of putting yourself out there, getting rejected, so most people who date you choose to do NOTHING but fuck and chill.

But the thing is, when you do not speak up about what you really want with someone, you usually never get what you want. They don't even know you want it! When you do nothing, you also get nothing.

Look, if you get to know someone and you like them enough to want to be in a relationship FULLY and officially, say so. Be blunt as hell. Be upfront as hell about it. You actually don't have anything to lose. Think about it: If you want to be official with someone and they want to be committed and exclusive with you, you win. If you want to be in a relationship with someone and they do not the same thing, you **STILL** win because now you know without a doubt where you stands in their life, where they stand in yours and can accept it without having to stick around to "prove your worth" or "make them see." They ALREADY see your worth and STILL don't want what you want. Let it go, or be strung along.

Be Clear: It's too vague to ask, "So... what are we... where is this going?" Be direct as hell. Chances are you want to know if you are "just getting to know each other" still "building a friendship" or if you are "dating exclusively." If you feel ready to stop dating other people, that is an appropriate time to ask if your "boo" is ready to do the same.

Friends First

Is it true that a person you get in a relationship with should be your friend first? It sounds nice, but what does it mean to be someone's *friend first* when you know damn well you don't have *"let's just be friends first"* emotions?

For one, friendships start with common interests and a strong comfortable vibe which leads to you dropping your guard and opening up. Next, you *naturally* become transparent and vulnerable because there is no ulterior motives or hidden agendas ... they genuinely care about you, not just what can you do for them. That's a real *natural* friendship and you never had to say *"let's just be friends first."* It just happened. I've found that the only real distinction between friend and boy/girlfriend is the attraction factor.

Men and women who are attracted to each other and who are mature do not *fake* platonic friendships for a few months so they can THEN be together. No, their bonding is built more on passion, flirting, and feelings. You can't hold back passion and play *"let's just chill"* if you know damn well you feel more than that. Yes, there are many instances where we hold back the passion because of bad timing and you become just friends due to those circumstance, but even then it's still understood—I don't want to be your homie, I'm only waiting for better timing to hook up.

marry your best friend.

When people come out and tell you that they married their best friend you can't take that to literally mean they started out just friends and it developed into more. No, they had some attraction towards each other. They started *dating*, getting to know each other and then learned more about each other AFTER they got together. Months and years of spending time together and learning new things about each other is how they became best friends. It's rare to be best friends first, THEN date. In reality, that **bestfriendship** develops over time.

My thing is this. We should not have to think *fake* we really feel just because society says being friends first is a better method. The question you should ask yourself is do you want to be somebody's friend right now or do you want to date because you have romantic feelings for them? As soon as you tell someone that you want to be their friend, you cancel out any *dating* for the moment. It's all about hanging out and chilling. Isn't that what you do with friends?

On the other hand, do you want to tell someone that you want to *date* them and get to know them? When you let them know that you want to go on *dates*, you are telling them that you are attracted to them. You are letting them know that you want to be friends, but you also see them in a more sexual light or think that they may be a candidate for a relationship, so you just want to get to know them better *that* way.

I think we have to be more realistic about this friend first thing we have in our society. Our Love Lives are not a sitcom on TV where you are friends for years and then all of a sudden fall for each other. Like all of this time you had zero attraction for each other, the friendship was purely platonic, but then you magically see something in them and want to marry them a week later. That's not how it goes. You *already like the person*. You are **ALREADY** aware of your feelings for this person before feeling like you are "friends first." Why do people make it seem like honesty, kindness and respect are only inherent in friendships, not in romance?

Too Much Too Soon

I am the type of person who gave a lot of themselves to the point of damaging my own circumstances. I use to frequently wrestle with the complicated feelings that came from giving too much too soon. For me, it was usually about the joy of the moment. But, the fear in my mind about possibly being taken advantage of had led to more pain than happiness. Also, the guilt of telling them "no", and most recently, the anxiety of feeling as though I have done more harm than good to a particular situation, has taught me a very valuable lesson: like everyone, my life was a work-in-progress to be more reserved and to learn how to save certain things about myself for a committed, interdependent relationship.

Meeting someone who suddenly makes you feel alive and loved is very exciting. You may think no one has ever made you feel like this and you can't help but be amazed at the chemistry, or electricity between you and this new love. Many people in relationships start this way. But sadly they don't take the time to get to know each other before jumping into something serious.

The truth is, this feeling of urgency and intensity or strong attraction toward another person is not necessarily a reliable indicator of whether you are in love or should immediately dive into a serious dating relationship. Most times you need to slow your ass down and access the situation. Time out. Sit down somewhere. Breath. Don't get too ahead of yourselves and throw EVERYTHING at a new person just because you like them. Or just because you are a *"naturally giving person."* Save some of that for a commitment.

When you slow your ass down before giving too much too soon, you are able to see more clearly whether they are right for you and you for them. This takes time. But, many people want to feel that rush of emotion that makes them feel like they are in love. So they push hard and quickly to feel that overwhelming emotion that says, I am in love. The obsess over proving their worth.

Over-giving Suffocates Love

It's like over-watering a plant. You want it to grow NOW. Your instincts tell you to nurture it, so you over-water it and kill it. Same for a relationship. The problem with over giving too soon is that you'll come across as needy and desperate, probably won't get enough back, so you'll feel cheated. You'll try harder to give more to prove your worth to get them to do it too. You'll be ignoring your own life to help them with theirs. He or she will take you for granted and expect you to continue to do more and more for them.

Kills The Challenge

You may have heard that making yourself too available too soon can damage a potential relationship because it takes away the challenge. Maybe you think that a past relationship failed because you were "too much." However, that might not be the case. In fact, if two people want to be in a secure relationship where both people feel safe to be vulnerable, then being available can bring them closer. Both people have to be ready, willing and able to give and receive love -- but when they're not, that's why the relationship fails.

When someone is dating or in a relationship, it is unattractive for them to be too available and that there needs to be a certain level of challenge in the relationship in order for the other person to remain interested and excited. Apparently, this is part of the reason so many of us go after the 'bad girls' or 'bad guys'. They keep the challenge exciting. Challenging means to be enough of assured person that you don't just go along with whatever the hell the other person says damn near every time. You have your own opinions, lifestyle, methodology that it "challenges" the other person's perspective. The only way we grow as people is to be challenged. The opposite of challenging is to just adapt to whatever likes/dislikes, lifestyles, and mannerisms of your partner. That's not healthy.

The thing is, if you're too available it means you may not have much else going on in your life... that's not attractive. Women are not into "bad boys" they're just not into "overly nice guys" aka "men that are doormats and will drop everything for her, every day, every time". They want men with a spine, a strong back bone, a man who can stand up for himself. Also, too many "nice guys" try to intentionally make themselves look too busy so that they don't seem to available. Never intentionally be a jerk, that's just screwed up. Why would you pretend to be busy? If you're never busy it's because you're probably not doing much of anything, get some hobbies, find a job, study, hang out with friends, etc. (example: I'm only available Wednesdays and Thursdays for women I've just met, weekends are for me, my friends and a girl I want to see romantically because we've been dating for some time.)

For men and women both, The problem is not being "too nice". The problem is being a doormat. Don't "pretend to be busy", actually have other things to do. Not being too available means that you have a life outside of the relationship and this life from time to time takes precedent over a man or woman.

Signs of Giving Too Much Too Soon

1. When I feel dependent on their validation of everything that I've done for them.
2. Usually when it feels like too much too soon, it is.
3. I'm increasing my effort just because I like them, not because they worked for it. It should be both at the same time.
4. They are telling me that they aren't ready, so I should slow the hell down before I push them away; not TRY HARDER.
5. I'm being too accommodating of their needs and ignoring my own. I'm unhappy trying to make them happy.
6. There is no commitment established but I feel like I'm in a relationship.... Sometimes.

At first, doing a considerable amount of things to impress each other and make each other extremely happy seems natural and even pleasurable. Think about it, when you like someone, doesn't it also make YOU feel good to do a lot of the things that makes them happy? After all, aren't we supposed to give our all if we really want someone? Well, in MY OPINION, at least not until we are truly in love or when dating reaches a certain point of trust and understanding; when the relationship is official.

I asked myself, why was I giving people so much of myself when they weren't officially MINE? My exaggerated effort was obviously pushing them away. I realized that doing too much too soon (giving my all to someone, BEFORE it was OFFICIAL) actually suffocated them and even myself. I concluded that giving too much too soon is by far the biggest pre-relationship mistake made by both men and women.

Too often people are left saying "but they changed!" No they didn't, you just finally found out who they really were. The truth came out. People can only put on a facade for so long, and if you make a permanent decision based on a temporary emotion, there is only pain to follow.

Availability Limits

Women pursue men in their own unique ways by making themselves available for us to make the first move. They place themselves where they will "catch our eyes". As a result, a man can drive a woman crazy by limiting his accessibility. One reason why he might be limiting his availability is because experience has taught him that a great deal of women *seem* to go for unavailable men. Sometimes, we even get into the habit of being "fake busy" so that we are not TOO available.

Based on the art of attraction, women learn to market themselves visually and men learn how to market themselves through their actions and possessions; having a job, money to date, a car to go places in, and ultimately having his own place. However, we all do not want to market ourselves to the point where we look too willing for anything or anyone. Experience has taught us that.

If you are always available, your time doesn't appear to be very valuable. If someone feels like you are going to make time for them out of your busy day, they will appreciate that time more. They do not appreciate your time as much if you have nothing else to do but talk and text them ALL damn day. You should not fake it though. If you really have that much of free time, you should find REAL things to keep you busy instead of creating illusions. Be authentic, not bogus. This way, it is real and not a game. The positive thing about staying busy by finding REAL things to do is that you'll have new things to talk about and you'll BE a more interesting person, and not SEEM like an interesting person.

Too Busy?

People who are "too busy" to see you are just that. They are too busy to see "YOU". Someone who really wants you will take time to see and contact you. Some people are either too lazy or not interested. Actually, it's not always about them NOT wanting you or NOT being interested in you. It may be a case of them not being interested *enough* to try harder to see you or talk to you. Reading this may sounds harsh if you do not want to accept someone's disinterest in you, but really, it probably has nothing to do with *you*. Maybe they are really focused on one thing or another and do not want to take the time to pay more attention to you. It is ok for them to have priorities other than you, right? My rule is this: If someone wants to see you they'll make time. Never get too involved with someone who tells you up front that they are too busy for you. I'm not saying that you should be petty about it. I am saying that avoiding those "too busy" people is for your own good. Nobody is too busy for a relationship if they really want to be in one.

If they don't call you It's because they do not want to call you. If they do not invite you to go out it's because they don't want to see you enough. If they treat you like shit it's because they do not care enough. If they let you go, they do not want to be with you enough. When someone says, "I love you but I'm not ready, now isn't the right time." It's simply because they don't want to put in the effort to love you better right now. Stop playing their mind games. Don't justify their bullshit. When one person wants to be with another, they'll stay without lies, excuses and complications. Relationships are only as complicated as people make them seem. It's simple, you want me? show me.

The reality of it all is that we put people into categories. When we think of certain people, we categorize them in this way:

a) People that I'll pay attention to whenever I find the time to ("Booty Calls" or New people)

b) People that I'll NEVER actually get with, but I'm either too shy or selfish to ever tell them — so I'll keep them around just to use them or until they fall back on their own (The Friend Zone)

c) People that I'll DROP EVERYTHING to get with — even if it means I'm actually REALLY busy, missing "turn up time" with my friends, or even missing out on some money. ("The Bae". People we feel a spark of deep chemistry with).

Now that you know this, the best thing for you to do is a to analyze your situation to identify which category you fit in. If you do not know, here's a suggestion:

If they treat you close to category A or B and nothing like C, then you might as well find a more available, willing, and more interested person to focus on.

"I'm too busy" is way too common of a cop-out in some relationships and has become more common and acceptable – hell, maybe even expected.

I think it is a sensible thing not to start a relationship if you feel you do not have the time to spend developing it.

If you are already in a relationship and your workload increases then you need to be honest with the other person, explain exactly what has happened, why you need to change your priorities, how long you except this to last and give a honest realistic promise of how much time you will have.

Fall Back Action

They say not to be "too available" and people take that as letting the phone ring longer than needed, not answering messages as soon as they receive them, or even pretending that their schedule is full. Isn't that considered "playing games"? Why fake your "fall back" just because you think that if you do not "fake" your availability, the other person will think that you are "clingy" or doing too much?

I hate when people pretend. Have you ever desired someone and initiated putting effort to get to know them, but they did not reciprocate the same effort? Even though they said that they wanted to get to know you, you still haven't seen any proof through their actions. In fact, it seems as if they were not even interested. But, you liked them. So, you tried not to call and text as much because you thought it would be better than "bothering" them with resent back to back messages. Next, you waited for them to contact you first because you did not want to seem desperate or clingy. You may have even decided to wait a few minutes to respond to texts just so you would not look too eager. Then after a while of no effort on their part, you just stop trying?

We try so hard to give off the impression that we are unavailable because we think that it is an effective technique to manipulate other people into pursing us. Also, we believe that if we limit our accessibility (fall back), we would not have to worry about pushing people away because we push ourselves away. We've all tried it, to make ourselves look unavailable so that the other person will increase their effort. Why do we do this? It all boils down to adjusting the "**demand curve**."

The **demand curve** is basically a measure of how much WE perceive that someone else will demand our time and effort. We believe that decreasing our availability will in turn, influence them to increase theirs. In other words, we supply less of ourselves while hoping that they will start demanding more and trying harder. We believe that adjusting the **demand curve** will work because life has taught us that we all want what or who we cannot have. I guess we subconsciously try to manipulate other people into wanting us.

There are many ways we try to accomplish mastering the **demand curve**. For some of us, we do not allow ourselves to be too common with anything that we do, or with any person of interest. We know that too much of anything is lame, basic and boring. Therefore, we choose to supply more of our time and effort, if they demand more; that is when we feel safe enough to open up. What we fail to realize about this **demand curve theory** is that we are only too eager to someone who is not ready for our type of love. The person that is meant for us will know how to handle us.

It's always a bad idea in my eyes to play the supply and demand game. First of all, playing games seldom works, except maybe in the short term. And second, someone who can only be won by playing games can generally only be kept by playing games.

Do yourself a favor, and don't bother with games. That way, you'll be able to attract someone who likes you when you're relaxed and just being yourself. Playing games is exhausting, and only one person can win at a time.

Are Nice Men Lame?

When we first meet a woman, we cannot expect her to give us everything just because WE believe we are good men. I know you've noticed that being a nice man does not always produce the best progress with women. Chemistry and compatibility are way more important than doing the things that we are supposed to do, anyway! The last time I checked, being nice, honest, and respectful is a part of being a decent human being. So, why would she reward you on being a good person? There are so many other elements that come into play that even a near "perfect" man cannot always overcome. Or at least won't always have the confidence to try to overcome. We are not entitled to shit these days. It is good to be nice to women, but what else can you do?

Just as some women give up everything before a commitment, men do the same thing. We give too much too soon while requiring the bare minimum or nothing In return; not even a commitment. If you treat a woman way better than you treat yourself, two things will happen: she will take advantage and use you, or you will become dependent on her; you "can't" be happy without her and her reciprocated effort. Both of those scenarios are bad. If you treat her way better than she treats herself, two things will happen: she will push you away into the friend zone, or SHE become dependent on you; she "can't" be happy unless YOU make her happy.

Good News: Your life isn't all about that woman. You shouldn't have to change yourself to the type of guys SHE likes just to impress her. It wouldn't be comfortable for you. You won't be showing your true self.

And THAT makes you lame.

You're not lame for being nice, you're lame for expecting rewards for being nice. Mom taught you to be nice regardless if you're going to get pussy in return. Regardless if you're going to get that date. Regardless if she texts you back. Regardless if she chooses her ex over you. If you expect rewards for your niceness, then you're a low-key jerk that's being nice just to sauce up some sex.

This doesn't mean **be a fake jerk** - purposely being distant and an asshole just because you think it will get you those digits or pussy ratings up. Being a jerk doesn't produce the best progress with women either. I honestly don't believe that women WANT jerks. But they wouldn't mind "fixing" them or changing them. They want the Challenge and excitement that comes with changing them, fixing them, or proving their worth to them. If you want a woman, challenge her. Give her excitement and adventures. Don't be a pussy. Most women like guys that they are dating to be a little "problematic". I mean a little naughty, challenging, dominating.

And the best standard for knowing if you are being too nice to women is when you find yourself in the "friendzone".

When you are a great guy, there's NOTHING to fix about you. You're already finished. You already like her without her having to excessively prove her worth to win you over. And if come across a woman who loves that challenge of proving her worth, she would think that you are boring because there is no excitement that **SHE** wants. Maybe you are exciting, just not her type of exciting. And even if you're not boring at all, that chemistry factor just isn't there because she likes that challenge. Jerks typically provide that.

Women probably HATE jerks and LOVE the challenge. So they put up with the bullshit of trying to get a jerk to want them willingly just to have that challenge rather than date a nice guy who is already willing to be hers without that challenge. I think they want a certain degree of aggressiveness, confidence, and of course sweetness every now and then too. Along with compatibility and creativeness with the way you carry yourself...

The Real Bad Guy

Advice men give men: "Man up." "Don't be a sissy." "Don't cry." "Talk like a man." "Act like a man." "Be a man." We absorb the words and then spend a lifetime dealing with their effects.

The REAL bad guy does not conform to society's bullshit. He says "NO" when it's appropriate. Society does not like him because he is too far in his own lane. Any person, place, or thing that proceeds to make his life hard, will be dismissed without a second thought. Most people are not used to this type of man, and that is why he appears to be a jerk for not putting up with their bullshit. His dedication to his personal growth may take up most of his time, and as a result, other people will think of him as being an inconsiderate jerk. Not only does he say "no" to women, he says no to anyone else who wastes his time. So, those men who lie and constantly cheat on women are not bad guys. Those liars and cheaters are pieces of shit. Women who lie and cheat on men are also pieces of shit. You can debate those last statements all you want.

If you want to do something but your girl wants to do something else, just tell her NO. Sometimes you can give up and do something she wants, but not all the damn time though. Don't lose yourself in trying to please someone else, because then she will not like who you become. Telling your girl no sometimes will keep her respecting you.

Telling a woman "no" means you are sure of yourself, you are not a lame and that she has to actually put in work in order to get to know you too. She does not want a "yes" man because after a while, they get boring. Telling her no sometimes means that she cannot throw pussy at you to get what she wants, then call it a day. She has to put in work in order to understand you.

It is not all about what we do. Sometimes, it is about what we DO NOT DO. We can no longer be inconsistent and complacent men. We have to put in work. Men who aspire to be husbands make sure that their women will never have to second guess their loyalty and trustworthiness. Do not be basic, be creative and interesting.

Becoming a better man is a choice and takes effort. We become better men when we display what we have learned from our mistakes and the mistakes of others. Also, we become better men when we use our experiences and observations to grow within ourselves and uplift others. Additionally, some of the most important things to do in order to be a better man consists of learning how to embrace our emotions, how to be considerate and how to feel comfortable being vulnerable.

We are taught that expressing our feelings makes us look weak. Society obliges to this fabricated idea of manhood through social media, music and television. The greatest contributors to this idea of manhood are our closest family members and friends. We are raised by the men in our families to value money, multiple women (while being taught to make sure women closest to us - sisters, cousins etc. - must keep their legs closed), cars, clothes, and even violence. We are taught by our friends (even female friends) that those materialistic things reflect our strengths, while expressing emotions, committing to one woman and showing love reveals our weakness. We wonder why we cannot see the value in what it truly means to be an open and expressive man because we do not know how to. Maybe the definition of being a man has changed over the years.

One thing that I have noticed is that we are still struggling with embracing the feelings that we try to hide. We invest so much of our time and energy into this deceitful idea of masculinity, that when it comes time to open up to women, we are afraid or do not have a clue how to.

Men Of Substance

Men of substance are compassionate and caring for all people. They respect others, remain loyal, and appreciate what people do for them. Men of substance strive to make the world a better place. They increase the quality of life, know right from wrong AND demonstrate it. They are focused on their goals and still find time to value the people and things around them. Men of substance do their best to prevent the end of good things and if you are not a part of their solutions, then they will consider you as a part of their problems. They will never let you forget how much they love you and take risks to achieve and sometimes they fail, but they never grow weary of trying. Simply put, men of substance put in work in all aspects of life and are HUMAN, in all of its wonderfulness.

To be a man of substance, do some substantial things. Don't waste your time pretending you are working extraordinarily hard on something but actually you are just wasting your time day by day.

What Do Men Want?

I cannot speak for all men, but based on the ones that I know, we all have VERY similar thoughts. However, even with parallel views, we all do not *ACT* on those thoughts in the same ways. With that being said, men fall into 3 categories:

1. **Men who just want to fuck.**
2. **Men who want a committed relationship (and sex). ****Usually the men of substance.***
3. **Men who want to be alone and single *(sex and friendships with women aka friends with benefits).***

Category: I Just Want To Fuck

If I just want to fuck you, I will most definitely only want your respect in the bed room. I will not care if you love me or not. If I just wanted the sex, I could care less about getting to know you. I may be a piece of shit in almost every other aspect in life, but that "dick" though, will have you ignoring all of my piece of shit qualities. As long as you fall in love with the sex, I'm going to love the "sex respect" that you show and continue throwing sex in your face because I see how much you appreciate the multiple orgasms. It does not stop there. I would not feel successful unless I get you to be loyal to me. I do not want to settle down with you, but I want to make sure that you do not give my pussy to anyone else. If my goal was to have sex and I liked it, chances are I want more sex with you. If I am this type of guy, then I'm damn sure not trying to be a man of substance and do not care for women at all. So, my perception of success is having sex and chasing multiple women, seeking respect from them homies, and making money. If I do not get money and multiple women, I will feel like a failure.

could settle down ANY day. The only time we stop or slow down is when we want to have sex and "chill," but *not* to settle down.

Little do we know, all women aren't distractions and relationships only get in the way of our success if we aren't committed to both our women and goals or if we date women who are full of shit. If we lose sight of other aspects in life, then we are distracting ourselves. If we keep our eyes on our values, we would end up both successful (including in marriage), happy and a good person, which is part of the recipe to be a man of substance.

Men Want Independent Women Too

You work hard, make your own money, and have your life nearly together. Also, you have your own mind. Nothing is more attractive than an independent woman who is powerfully expressive. Why would we not want you? If you can teach me something new, life together will be a lot more interesting as I also teach you new things along the way. Unfortunately, some independent women do not believe that men want them.

One thing that I know for a fact is that a lot of women are stuck with the belief that men do not adore independent women. While there are a great deal of insecure men who cannot handle working women, in many other cases men LOVE boss women. However, one reason why men may not pursue some independent women is because SOME of them are always broadcasting how much they DON'T need a man. Bragging is unattractive for any human being. We get it, you are proud and focused. The thing is, we are not actually looking for independent women who want to do everything by themselves, we want the ones who are independent, but value doing things WITH us.

The truth is, we already know damn well that you may not need a man, but we also know that you want one. So, by all means, be all about your independence, just don't forget to let us know that you also want a committed relationship too.

Maybe you feel as though he wants to control you or make you STOP making more money than him. That is not what a man of substances wants. Putting his comfort above your own SOMETIMES in the relationship to make him happy doesn't mean you have to ALWAYS sacrifice your wants or needs. The sacrifices are usually small and are actually in the form of healthy compromising and cooperating. Making HIM feel comfortable means that you're excited about having him in your life and that you genuinely believe he is deserving of your time and love. On top of that, you know that he would make those same sacrifices for you.

Gentlewoman Checklist

1) Women who value their bodies, time, energy and minds; Loyal, appreciative, ambitious, mentally and emotionally stable.
2) A woman who knows how to pleasure a man and can get turned on by turning him on.
3) Women who dress up for us.
4) *Interesting without being impossible to figure out.*
5) Helps him build a relationship that is full of *peace*.
6) A woman who appreciates him and finds more reasons to love and less reasons to complain.
7) A woman who won't embarrass him because she can handle herself. She gets alone with others.
8) A woman who knows how to prepare a good meal. (Even if he can cook too.)
9) Supportive.
10) *Sex*. Do not act like you did not know this.

The Male Perspective

We apply our flawed perception of value to a woman that we entertain based on how much we believe that she value herself. If she has been giving us all of "her" while requiring nothing or little in return, then that tells us how much she values herself and we know she'll settle for the less that we give. The type of women that throw EVERYTHING at us too soon aren't the ones we want to settle down with. But they are usually the ones we wouldn't hesitate to mess around with.

These are some of the traits men look for, but these aren't always what we settle for. Just like some women, we also settle for less sometimes.

***Cooking and cleaning for us is extra.
We are grown. We can do those things
ourselves. We aren't looking for moms to
baby us or take care of us.

1. Is this woman going to make my life hard? Does my life feel better with her or without?
2. Is this woman going to try to change me? Can I be ME freely without her complaining?
3. ***Amazing Sex***
4. Thot Fax = is she known for fucking the homies, club promoters, guys on the block, rappers, brothers, cousins. Do I have to constantly hear the "You know she fucked so and so" story from multiple people who I didn't even ask?
5. Do I have to be her man in order to get all of these benefits, or do they come free?
6. Is her curve game extremely strong and brutal when it comes to other men trying to get at her? Will she QUICKLY dismiss any guy that's obviously trying to flirt or get with her.
7. Basics = ambitious, respectful, honest, independence, loyalty,

trustworthiness etc.
8.   Is there a "spark".
9.   Am I afraid of losing her?
10. Does she love herself?
11. Does she love me?
12. Am I in love with her?
13. Emotional, mental health.
14. Is she comparing me to who I was yesterday, or to her irrelevant exes?

Stop Trying to Change a Man that Does Not WANT to Change for YOU

Often finding yourself catering to men who aren't official with you? Those women are hoping to get these men to commit to them if only these men could "see their worth." Either that, or they try to force men to date them. I say "force" because, from a male's perspective, it feels like they are making it mandatory for us to transform into the way that THEY want us to be. The final straw is when they hit us with ultimatums.

No one likes being forced to do shit.. No matter how well you cook, clean and sex a man, he is going to choose the woman he wants to be with on his own because he doesn't want anyone else when he feels ready. A man that is sure of the woman he wants does not want to ever risk losing. As simple as that. You cannot make us WANT to change.

We will continue to treat you the same way because we do not see the benefit or joy in being the same way that YOU want us to. Therefore, you should leave a man before you try to change a man, because that man has been living a particular way because he wants to. Proving your worth cannot change what he wants.

Furthermore, we think that it is quite selfish of you to force us to change, just to make YOU happy. So, we'd rather leave you alone than to become a different person for you. Always remember, if we do not change, it is because most times we love being the way that we already are. We'll listen to what you want from us but if we don't WANT that or love you, we are not going to take any of those you seriously.

If we "ain't shit" for treating you how we want to treat you, then you ain't shit for staying. Why do you want us to change? Is it because it'll make YOU happier? You mean to tell me that the only reason you are here is because you want US to make you happy? Trying to get us to change doesn't make US happy.

You just have to learn to not try to change a man from one mindset to another. If I am just looking for sex, and I tell you I that I do not want anything serious, please don't waste your time trying to convince me.

Sometimes, that need to prove your worth is what drives the "I do not want to change" men away. My opinion is that you should date the man who's looking for what you want and things will work out.

No matter how many different ways that I say this, it all means the same thing: wanting us to change for you, means wanting us to stop doing what we WANT to do, and stop being who we like to be, just to make YOU happier. Horacio Jones

Even if what we like to do is bad and dead ass wrong, we still WANT to do it. You have a choice to put up with it. Instead of trying to change everyone you date, just so YOU can be happy, how about you learn how to let people be themselves, and leave them the fuck alone if you can't handle it or respect it? All you can do is bring awareness to how they do not appreciate women because it is not your job to change them.

We have to change ourselves. Forcing us will not be pleasant for you or us. Yeah, we will "try" for a few days, but what does that mean to us if it is not something that we WANT to do consistently? At the end of the day, men who are forced into relationships or to change will still find ways to do their slick shit on the side. In order to not look like the bad guy, we would rather make you look crazy. So, let us be us, and if you do not like it, leave because we still have a lot of growing up to do.

Super Hero Man

I am a recovering Super Hero. I ruined many friendships and potential relationships by "heroically" swooping in when my female friends were having problems. My shoulder was always soaked in tears and right before I'd dry it, they would go back to their exes. Or, they would end up in my bed for a couple of one-night stands. Then, they would wake up feeling saved and ready to love again... to love their exes again. It took me a very long time to realize that I was "saving" these women so that they could run right back to the villains. However, I have recently retired my cape because in reality, I can only save myself.

Some men have adopted the idea that they are supposed to be the "hero" in a stressed and broken woman's life, because she needs saving from herself and from "Bad Men." They enforce the "Save-A-Hoe" code of chivalry and use old-fashioned graciousness and sweetness as their secret weapons. They are fascinated by women in distress, depressed, needy or damaged. The super hero man is convinced that he can "save" these women, fix them, and then date them.

These women all share the same stories and characters: they've been cheated on, treated like shit by their exes, they have emotional issues, and maybe even history of abuse. The only way to be content, Captain-Save-A-Hoe senses the NEED to save one (or all) of these women. Therefore, he internalizes an exaggeratedly unrealistic and glamorized idea of the women he attends to, and sees them as hopeless and worthy of his heroics and love.

Unfortunately, every hero has their downfall. Eventually the Super Hero Men realizes that the only people they can save are themselves. Instead of inheriting a woman's pain, he learns how to be there for her while she SAVES HERSELF. The beauty behind dating a woman that has saved herself is that she will KNOW how to love you unconditionally. She does not want to be saved.

The WOSRT MEN ON EARTH

Manipulators always have hidden agendas and ulterior motives. They ALWAYS have concealed reasons for doing something that is different from the stated or apparent reason. If you have an ulterior motive for doing something, you do it partly because you think you will get some advantage from doing it. When a man's effort or support to a woman comes with hidden agendas, a line gets crossed. He is no longer hoping that she will recover from her past. His goal is not to love her. Instead, it is to win her over, exploit her and to be rewarded with sex for all of his efforts. Some men will actually take an active role, turning themselves into a combination of a caring and selfish shoulder for her to depend on. How do you think women would feel about men whose idea of dating includes persuading women to feel obligated to have sex with them?

The main thing about these Manipulators: they tend to be the FOULEST ASSHOLES. They consciously pray on broken women, because they do not think that they can get a well put together woman. So, they pray on women in distress, hoping to "*save*" them, expecting a reward. Sadly, some women are too vulnerable to realize what these men are doing to them.

But wouldn't women appreciate a guy who appears to treat\ them with respect, one who has a sense of empathy and compassion? A guy who wants nothing but the best for them? Is there really anything wrong with that? Well... How do you think women would feel about a guy whose idea of a healthy relationship involves making women to feel a sense of obligation to them?

As long as they get what they want, they are satisfied enough to be able to handle knowing that they have further damaged another woman in the process. By manipulating a woman, he overwhelms her with fake personality and she rewards him with her body. The simple fact that he uses manipulation rather than genuine love automatically makes him the worse type of guy on earth.

The Friend Zone

There are good men and women who do not get the kind of treatment from the woman/man that they want or think that they "deserve." Regardless of how good or bad we are to our significant other, two things that we cannot force are chemistry and compatibility.

The friend zone isn't always a bad place to be. Being "friend zoned" means that not everyone is meant to be with who they want. Misunderstanding the friend zone might be the problem with a lot of people today. We need to stop trying to force things because we feel it is right, and let things happen when they happen. The challenge is to remain that good friend after the fact and keep the truthfulness of who we are, intact. What's meant to be will always be. There is no denying that it is easier to say you've been FRIENDZONED, as if it is the other person's fault, than admitting you are not who they want.

DO SOMETHING DIFFERENT

Women desire other men because other men are interesting and different. Those interesting men do not make themselves TOO available. They do not give women all of the benefits of a relationship just because they like them. Instead, they make women earn it. Simply put, their life does not revolve around pleasing and doing EVERYTHING to seem completely in love with a woman that they're just dating.

We can get out of the friend zone by making ourselves better, more interesting people. When they distance themselves from us and keep us as friends, we should stop writing it off as being friendzoned. We should stop blaming them when our approach or timing may have been the problem. Sometimes, they're just not that into us. Other times, they are actually looking out for us because they truly might not be ready for what we want to offer. They may still be hurting and do not want to hurt us.

Instead of focusing on women's behavior, we should ask ourselves why are we attracted to women who pull away? What is the perception about ourselves or love that would cause us to recreate these same "friendzone relationships" with women? Maybe we feel as if it is safer to chase unavailable women because we'll never get close to them, and doubt that we are worthy of good available women. Maybe it is time that we do something different.

Friend Zone Entry Guide for Men

Stop Complaining, start understanding. You see, we fail because we come on entirely too strong, too fast, too early. After a couple of dates, we damn near try to marry these women. We have to remember that just because we are nice guys, that doesn't mean we are the right guys.

Being respectful and sweet does not separate us at all these days, and they do not have an award for saving broken people who haven't saved themselves yet. At the end of the day, she wants an adventure, not just sexual ones either. How creative can you be? She is attracted to innovative, confident and ambitious men. How hard are you working to build yourself? She is attracted to men who aren't lazy bums. Also, it is about SWAG = your physical features and how well you dress them, the words you use and how you present your intelligence consistently. So, how well do you finesse your appearance, Bruh?

The main way into the friendzone is by not making your intentions clear, letting her vent all damn day about other men, trying way too hard (being EXTRA), and by being afraid of rejection.

The most important thing you need to know is that most men get "friend-zoned" because those women were not sexually attracted to the them. They can try as hard as they want, but 99% of the time, "trying harder" becomes annoying and certain women would rather push those "die hard" men away. A woman either wants you or she doesn't.

She's Just Not That into You

Like men, women have their own preferences. I am convinced that a woman's idea of the "ideal man" is surprising even to her. However, some men do not get the hint when she rejects HIS idea of an ideal man. Let's get this straight, you are not stuck in the friend zone. You only get stuck somewhere if you accept it. Your game has to be tight or you just have to take the rejection like a man and leave her alone.

Do not be thirsty. The only guys in the friend zone are the ones who choose to stay there. All you have to do is NOT BE:

A. Whack
B. Extra
C. Corny
D. Weird

But if you ARE...... Opt out IMMEDIATELY.

She's Just Not That into You.

Why "Nice Guys" Finish Last

"Nice guys finish last" is a cop out a lot of brutally codependent men use. They start a relationship and base their own happiness on their woman's happiness and wants. This will eventually go south. The "nice guy" will either begin to resent her because he starts to feel he isn't being rewarded or recognized enough for his efforts or, she will begin to feel smothered and once this feeling gets to a certain level, she will ask for space or just end it. This is when the clingy guy tells everyone how he was used and **"nice guys always finish last."**

Striving to always "be nice" instead of REAL makes you just a "friend" or "too good to be true. Smothering. Clingy. Predictable + No Excitement = Unappealing and BORING."

Balance and self-respect are your friends, don't leave them behind when you meet a woman. As soon as you STOP living a full life, due to limiting it so it can resolve all around her, and stop putting forth REAL hardworking effort to improve yourself as an individual because you are too wrapped up into her or afraid to lose her, this is when you become less interesting as A MAN. It's not because you're too nice. It's because AS A MAN: you no longer have anything to offer to her in terms of growth outside of her. It just looks like you have no life outside of her.

Women are drawn to full lives; men who are living life and building. They don't want to be the only thing you work for. Men who still make and keep plans with family and friends, attend events/activities to grow in some way, have fun activities going on in their lives of THEIR OWN- all of these indicate BALANCE. Everyone feels good inside to be on balanced space and it presents a picture of a life that makes a woman from the outside looking in want to be a part of it. This is why when your entire purpose centers around the woman, she begins to pull away because she loses interest. She sees herself in literally everything you do and that's not always interesting.

1. "Nice Guys" finish last because they do not set boundaries or make any demands. They are so into the women who they date, that they neglect themselves to the point of allowing women to control them. Jerks on the other hand, do not let women control them.

2. Some women confuse controlling and demanding jerks with men who are confident. Those same women confuse "nice guys" as push overs.

3. Nice guys are predictable. They repeat the same nice guy behaviors because it worked the first time and they are afraid to try something different. They fear that their women would leave them if they took risks and fail. Little do they know, women are attracted to spontaneous men who offer excitement and challenges. Compared to dating nice guys, dating "jerks" is always a project for women who love trying to prove their worth. Nice guys let women wrap them around their fingers ASAP.

4. Most "nice guys" aren't being real and are too agreeable, so women assume that these men are too good to be true. Jerks "keep it real," while nice guys do not want to upset their women ever.

5. Nice guys rarely need to be saved and some women like to "save" men. They end up trying to save "jerks" because they think their love will save them.

6. "Jerks" become projects to reach their "potential". Some women do not want to "open up" but, a nice guy will eventually want a commitment from them too soon.

BROKEN VISION

Why do most women dislike the word "friendzone"?

Because it implies a thoughtful choice, or conscious effort to put a guy there when in reality, she's just not interested in him LIKE THAT. It implies that the woman is actively choosing to not be sexually attracted to the guy who is doing "all the right things" for her, when in truth, attraction is an emotion, and she has no more control over it than if she feels happy or sad.

As men, we would sit there like, "How dare you not be attracted to me? I did everything for you, blah blah blah...!" not realizing that THAT'S why she's not interested. Just because we're attracted to a woman, that doesn't mean she is attracted to us, nor does it mean she has to be.

I have never been able to choose who I'm attracted to. If I'm not attracted to you but like you as a person, I may want to be friends with you. If you can't handle being friends with me, then say so. Don't stick around hoping one day I'll get the hint. If I am not attracted to you at the start, there is a chance that it will never happen. Or maybe things will randomly spark up. Who knows? But when the spark isn't initially there, the motivation to "manually" spark things up between us isn't there either.

However, it is quite simple: If I'm not attracted to you, I'm just not. There isn't much either of us can do about it, it's just the way things are. Using the term 'friendzone' to describe a natural function I have no control over is really unfair. Maybe things can change, but I won't force it. So, with that logic, I see why women hate the word "friend zone." I hate when women say that I friend zoned them.

I USED to think I was friend zone by someone. Then I realized 2 things:
1. But believe it or not, "Friendship" is a suitable relationship status when you're dealing with a woman who doesn't want anything serious..
2. That women either liked me or they didn't. That's how the cookie crumbles.

Now, I have little sympathy for someone complaining about being in the "friend zone." Having feelings for someone doesn't mean they will be reciprocated, and a lot of us have to learn that the hard way.

If someone is direct with you about not being interested, they have taken care of their responsibility by being upfront. If they are really upfront, they may tell you things that turned them off and ways you could improve yourself, but not for them, they rather help you meet someone new.

Every time I hear someone say "friend zone", I just picture a guy liking a woman and is really nice to her, so he feel entitled to reciprocal romantic interest from her. My question is, why can't a friendship with a woman be valued or worth pursuing? I mean, do you HAVE to date her?

The term Friendzone was kind of amusing for about the first 30 billion times it was used AS A JOKE!

Friend Zone Avoidance Notes:

1. **Women do not feel comfortable with people who treat them better than they treat themselves when they have low self-esteem.**
2. **Relax and take it moment to moment.**
3. **Tease her.**
4. **Make her laugh.**
5. **Challenge her.**
6. **Express your opinions.**
7. **Do not be afraid to disagree.**
8. **Do not be extra: not too available, not too unavailable.**
9. **Rejection does not mean try harder. Being rejected usually means that you should stop trying or try something different.**

The Compatibility Spark

Imagine a woman in a relationship with a man that she defined as respectful, emotionally available, amusing, and good in bed. She loved him, but was not *in love* with him and did not see a future with him. The reason why she stayed so long was because he was a good man. Unfortunately, she did not feel a Spark with him. When asked what specific recipe made her feel a spark, she said that she could not explain it. She felt as though she was settling for less without the chemistry. So, she left him because "something was missing."

Would you date someone you were not attracted to? Most people would say no. They would choose to kindly abandon the other person before that person's feelings grew any stronger. I personally would rather be single than in a relationship that is passionless and mind-numbing even when sex is involved. It takes more than great sex to build a successful relationship, but sex seems to be my generation's foundational first steps for relationship building. When one person feels the spark and the other doesn't, usually the sex is better than the bond. Either way, the result is still an awkward break up.

If you know that someone is into you, doesn't it suck when they want you to return the same level of attraction when you aren't as enthusiastic about it as they are? Even when you think that they are a sweet person, don't you find it difficult to explain how you just do not "feel it" with them? When you date good people and enjoy it, but do not feel any real desire with them, you get jammed. Your options are:

1. leave a really good person,
2. Or understand that they have most of the qualities that you are looking for in a mate and maybe you could build a spark with them over time.

Sometimes, the initial spark and chemistry fades over time. It took me a long time to accept that some relationships grow stronger and eventually evolve, while others burn out and fade away. I really think that in order for the relationship to last, the Spark needs to be replaced with security and trust after years of being with a person. I know that's not as exhilarating, but it is soothing in its own right, and more than enough for me. When you love someone, no matter how much time has passed, you will find creative ways to show it and appreciate the good relationship. I will take security over a spark any day.

I guess what I'm trying to say is that the spark isn't everything and in the end, you need to see if you can wake up every morning next to that person and feel secure and loved. Sometimes, it takes a little effort and creativity to keep things fresh and exciting, but the result is more than worth it.

Naïve Sparks

Nowadays, it seems as though the "Spark" decides who we date. It is not that they do not want YOU, they want someone with those qualities PLUS THE SPARK and chemistry. Understand this, you have "A" SPARK, but not "THE SPARK", and they cannot imagine going out with someone for whom they felt no natural interest. So, they 'friend zoned' you, not to be an asshole, but because you are a good person and they actually like your **friendship**. However, even though they like you, they do not have romantic feelings towards you.

Can a relationship grow a spark?

Yes. Will it ever feel as powerful as a natural build? You never know. Can you form something with someone you do not feel a spark with? Of course. However, it is not easy because you feel as though you are "**forcing**" yourself to date.

Dating solely based on lustful sparks is a misconception of the mind and why relationships seem to not grow. The Spark (familiarity through chemistry - which is usually desired subconscious patterns) alone, does not make relationships and basing relationship choices on a "feeling" isn't enough. What about trust? What about respect? Just because you have that strong feeling doesn't make them the "right person," and just because you do not feel the Spark initially doesn't mean it cannot grow.

No spark or chemistry are our code words for *"I know what I want, but I'm going off what I naturally feel."* If you only date people who you feel a natural spark of chemistry with, maybe you need to figure out why in the hell you only feel sparks and chemistry with people who play games with you. If trying to change someone who you feel a spark with hasn't been working out, why not try appreciating a better person who you can create a new spark with? Especially if the sparks you've naturally felt have lead you down hurtful paths. What if the REAL challenge is learning how accept what is better for you, rather than trying to change someone into what you "deserve"? You do not want to "force" yourself to like someone, but you've been "forcing" someone else to treat you better. Think about that.

Textationships

In today's dating world, people will think that you do not like them if you do not text back fast enough. If you do not text back, they will get pissed off. Instead of calling you, they will just wait, mad as hell all day, for you to respond. It makes me sick.

We are lazy and texting is easy. On top of that, we are catching feelings through texts, so there's no effort or urge for calling and meeting up. Instead of expressing our deepest thoughts in person, we do it through text because it's laid-back. It is easy to click through text messages. It barely requires any real effort. That's why so many relationships can go wrong especially if one person is too lazy to communicate properly in person; we only know their "text personality".

Also, people are very shy and do not have the courage to speak face to face. When you are texting, you have time to think about what you want to say and think about how the other person will perceive your message. So in reality, they are getting an edited, filtered, and too thought out version of what you think they want you to be. In person, the interaction is unedited and unfiltered; you do not have time to think long and hard about a response. So, the person gets to see more of the real you.

Additionally, texting has taken intimacy away from us; it has no emotion. I think it robs us of real, genuine conversations. It also robs us of quality time spent in person. They cannot see real facial expressions through text. They cannot physically see if you are actually laughing your ass off. They can only imagine it. In person, there are no misinterpretations or emotionless replies just because they sound like good responses.

Too much texting, not enough dates.

Our dating culture has evolved to a cycle of text messages, rather than doing a dinner and a movie. Most people now would rather exchange texts, Facebook posts, instant messages, DMs, etc. instead of actually going out. I mean sure, we can have a great conversation via text, but the deepest and dopest conversations happen face to face, over drinks in the dark corner or a lounge. Sadly, now emoji flirting is the new first date.

Don't Text Me

If we do not call or see each other, there's only so far we can go. If you can only express yourself through texts, but not through other means of communication, you're not interesting enough to hold my attention. I'll express how much I hate texting and tell people to call me. Then they will try to hold long text conversations anyway. If you want someone, CALL them and go see them. I'm not in the mode to try to spark up a full blown relationship through text. I can't be that Textationship guy in the real world.

Look, when you settle for those Textationships, you're just falling for the words of someone rather than the actions. You're falling for the picture that is being painted for you. The words are what attracts you to them, but it's the actions that will actually move you closer. Remember, anyone can tell you want you want to hear, but everyone can't back up what they speak of. Now that you are intrigued by those TEXTS, you should spend some time with that person, so they can put those words to action.

Do Not Stop Loving

Do not stop loving. Instead, you should start loving for YOU. Use love to redefine your status as an individual that is disconnected from the source of your pain. When you love and live for YOU, the source of your pain transfigures into the loneliness and disconnectedness that only you can work on. The source of your pain will no longer be the person who betrayed you, it will be the void that is left after a break up. What is better than filling that void with SELF-LOVE? It is a difficult process that I've been dealing with, but what I did was NOT stop loving myself. I did not want to stop loving anyone. I choose to still be happy without having to be with anyone but myself first.

We should also continue loving other people. The reason why we should not try so hard to stop loving people is because the love that we have for them is a reminder of the beautiful times in our lives. That love shows us how strong our hearts are.

"No Love Lost" has helped me forgive my ex. The goal was not to stop loving her, it was to accept my love for her while also accepting that I could not be with her for my own good. FOR MY OWN GOOD. Key word: GOOD. It is good for us to love, even if we cannot have them. Love keeps us alive. The pain from lack of acceptance is what kill us.

A part of acceptance is letting go of the 'what ifs' and realizing the value we have in this world as individuals. After the difficult process of detaching yourself from someone, it is a beautiful feeling to still be able to love them from a far and accept that the happiness you seek is truly found within yourself. When you accept the outcome in the form of love, you can look back without crying and recall memories without them hurting. Through acceptance, you release yourself from shackles of hurt and pain. With love, you maintain the ability to move on to someone new.

HORACIO JONES

STILL Busy???

If you are too busy to date, then you are certainly too busy to nurture a fun and healthy relationship. In other words, even if you somehow stumbled across someone who wanted to date you, they'd probably end up annoyed and frustrated about your unavailability and just cut you off.

"Busyness" is most often an illusion. Is a romantic relationship important to you? Then make time for one. How about you try to adjust your time according to your priorities? Real priorities. Significant ones. Maybe you are in a situation where you cannot afford to spend less time at work, school etc. Maybe you need to work multiple jobs, you have kids and taking care of a parent, to put food on the table, for example. In that case, a romantic relationship is most likely not going to happen right now, unless you MAKE TIME. If a happy, free and fun relationship is what you want, maybe it's time to work on changing your life so it can happen someday. You become a very annoying person when you claim to be so busy, yet you're still out trying to halfway date people, while they want to fully date you. If you're "too busy" working on you, then go finish doing that.

Stuck

Sometimes I felt stuck. I knew I could not have who I truly wanted. I tried to put up with the bullshit for the sake of our long history. But we simply could not find a way to make things work. I walked out, but my heart stayed... Stuck... And when I thought it was "all said and done", I'd always think of more things to say, and those words would always lead to more things I wanted to do against my worth. It is like, even when you try your best to move on, it is hard to open up to someone else because deep down inside, you really do not want anyone else. You're stuck.

Horacio Jones

If you're wondering how to manipulate your way out of "the friend zone", stop wondering. If they aren't interested, they aren't interested.

*Is it really that difficult to find
someone who truly loves you?*

It is difficult to find someone who
truly love you *the way you want
to be loved.*

People love you the best way
they can, and sometimes that just
isn't enough.

Just Do It

Our words can often interfere with our own actions. There is always more said than done. The proof is not in our words, but in our actions. What's the point in saying we'll do something when we can just do it?

It is easy to say "I will change" or "I will treat you better" but it is much more difficult to actually show that on a consistent basis, and a lot of times, it is difficult to even notice that "change." That's why we have things like #Wcw #MCM #RelationshipGoals #HisAndHers to encourage us to show false representations of the state of our relationships instead of actually having a solid relationship with one another, not worrying about what other people think or how they see our relationships.

No one needs to know that you are going to the gym, just go. You do not need to #Instagram your #MCM every week, WE KNOW, just physically show HIM. You do not have to post your food, just eat it. Less people care than you think, and all they really want to do is find something wrong with you or with what you do. Our lives do not improve by being on display, it improves when we take the steps to improve it. No more talking or fake posting, just do what you need to do. It'll be valued more.

Call Me Crazy

I had let my passion go, and a bit of my sanity went with it. I had lost my grip. I was so obsessed with finding out the truth, that I started doing things that only made me look even crazier than I already thought I was. Love did not do that to me, being naive, not trusting what was in my face and doubting my intuition, did that to me. Horacio Jones

I tried to stop the cheating and lying by shifting far outside of my element. I was checking phones, stalking social media, and I got really jealous. That's when I surrendered to my passion, and really appeared senseless and irrational. I was so obsessed with finding out the truth, that I began doing things that only compelled others to think that I was truly going crazy... and when she'd say "you are tripping" I'd stop and evaluate what the fuck I was doing. I was really feeling like I was going crazy. I was trying to MAKE this grown ass woman be honest. All of that energy wasted, and all I had to do was leave, accept that she was lying on purpose, she WANTED to lie, I could not change her, and no matter how much I tried to manipulate the situations, she would lie anyways. Just when I felt sure that she was lying, she would find a way to embarrass me and throw me off. The hardest thing to do was stay away. But that got easier over time. I did not want anyone calling me crazy anymore. I reminded myself that I was a grown ass man. So why the hell was I letting this woman make me feel less than that?

The "You're Crazy" Phrase

Certain people call you "crazy" because it is a defense mechanism that they use to minimize your feelings so that they can control you. In order for them to continue being sneaky, they need to make sure that you no longer trust your own feelings and instincts. They want to make sure that you rely on them to tell you how you are supposed to feel. They call you crazy so that you won't trust your own intuition. The funny part about letting them call you crazy is that you'd actually look back at all of the things you've done, feeling embarrassed and ashamed. Then you will start to rethink everything, as if you did it out of craziness. Well, if they can stop you from trusting what you feel, they will make you trust what they say you should feel, and they said you are crazy. So, what are you?

How to make someone look crazy:

1. Your sex game needs to exceed your character and personality. Do this by setting the bar low with your behavior, so that you have room for improvement. Therefore, giving them hope that things will get better. Meanwhile, you can continue pulling them back in with orgasms every time they say "I'm done with you."

2. Have random spurts of corrected behavior, demonstrating that you have the ability to be a better partner for them. Therefore, having them fall in love with your potential.

3. Flirt heavily with other people, and accuse your partner of being overly insecure and jealous.

4. Never answer phone calls around them. Never let them see your phone screen. Change your passwords often. Delete your texts and call logs. They will become increasingly curious and start their investigations into your phone, social media, and other people you know.

5. NEVER GET CAUGHT CHEATING. Only "almost" get caught. Just enough to make them want you to not have any opposite sex friends. They may even be skeptical about your family.

6. Disappear for hours or days without communication.

Now that you know the method of making someone look crazy, you now know how NOT to get fooled. The goal should be to stop letting people tell you how to feel. On the other hand, some people get really desperate for the truth. So they start doing things irrationally. Which makes them really look crazy. Sometimes, it is not even about the other person, it is about controlling yourself and getting a grip. Chill out.

***Declining someone else's emotional state is a way of directing them away from the truth. If they no longer have confidence in their own feelings, they'll end up relying on someone else to tell them how they should feel.

The Crazy Ex

After breaking up, one of the hardest things to do is to leave your ex the hell alone. Regardless of who dumped who, sometimes you still want them back. You want them back so badly that you will have a thousand and one things to say to them, then become obsessed with trying to get them to forgive you or want YOU back. Desperate times calls for desperate measures though, right?

I used to try to convince her that she was wrong about breaking up, and to give our relationship a second chance. My mind would fill with great things to say. Then, I'd feel like shit when my ex kept avoiding those talks that I had been desperately wanting. What I did not realize was that my ex had decided to ignore me and that I at least owed her that freedom. Calling, texting and repeatedly trying to make contact, only made things worse.

At first, it made sense in my mind; I wanted her to know that I still desired her. I wanted her to know that I was thinking about her no matter what we've been through. I wanted her to see how much effort I was putting in, so that she may all of a sudden want to do the same. But, it did not work most times. In fact, she ended up pushing me away.

She saw my texts. My missed calls were being viewed. She saw my emails and my indirect Instagram posts that were actually making things worse. She saw me. She just did not want to deal with me at that time because she felt as though I was doing wayyyyyy too much.

I tried not to worry about my ex not calling or answering me after a break up. I get it.... Someone who breaks up with me is going to feel awkward talking to me for a little while, and they want space. It is always best to calm my ass down, so they can at least have the chance to miss me, need me, and want me again.

However, my ex could not possibly miss me if I was still trying to get in touch with her. Which is why nothing I seemed to have done, worked. In fact, the harder I tried, the faster she would run. I realized that my best bet was to leave her the hell alone with her thoughts so that she could have a little time and breathing room. Every time I invaded that breathing room, I looked "crazy."

How to Stop Being Crazy

The first thing that I needed to do was stop inventing reasons to contact her. I had to stop trying to make up reasons to go to her house. Why? Because what I really was going to end up doing was convince her into ANOTHER sit down "let's get back together" talk. My actions were completely counterproductive because I was sabotaging my future chances by constantly bombarding her with relationship talk, which she was trying to stay away from. I was postponing the REAL deep conversation that she would have actually wanted, AFTER I calmed the hell down and AFTER she had felt ready (Sometimes they will never be ready, so you can't wait forever. You better get the hint).

Second thing I had to do was let her call ME when she was ready to talk. I learned that minding my own business until she sought me out would have shown me that she was thinking of me and was ready to discuss things. I did not say WAIT for her, I said that I minded my own damn business and worked on myself.

One thing is for sure, I am not waiting forever for anyone. Before she called me, I proceeded to cut all ties and communication. After that, the next thing I know, my ex was calling me just to see how things were going on my end. It was the way that I handled those "come back calls" that determined whether or not I was making myself look crazy. Usually, I would instantly start accusing her of lying and using me for money. I looked crazy because I never had proof. Over time, I had to learn that sometimes that "come back call" is truly and only just to check up on you and not to leap right back into a relationship. You will ruin a sweet conversation with someone you really care for by bombarding them with relationship talks every time they call you. Chill out... do not force it.

Trying to force her to get back with me was all wishful thinking, with the real end result in the form of shame. The day will come when you will realize that you pushed them into a corner during a break up, and instead of wanting to work things out, they will truly think you are crazy. Whatever you do, keep your dignity. Just relax, If they want space, you owe them that.

People go back to what
they knew and what they
are comfortable with even
when it wasn't good for
them because at least
they already know what
to expect with that person
and they haven't decided
to be alone and happy.

Most people will
say that they run
back because of the
love, but it's really for
comfort. Since when
did love become the
only reason to be with
someone?

The real you is revealed
every time you
do what you claim you
wouldn't do anymore.

-        horaciojones

Find someone you're
willing to grow for...
Start with yourself.
Build yourself, prove
your worth to yourself,
support yourself,
value yourself and
love yourself so much
that putting your heart
back on the line again
doesn't feel like a risk.
But instead, it'll feel like
an opportunity for self-love
and someone else's love.

\-   Horacio Jones

You'll always question if leaving is the right decision. You'll never really be sure of what's on the other side of the door once you walk out and close it. Just remember, it's not always about the single life that you're walking into, it is also about knowing and understanding what you are walking away from.

HoracioJones

The Confirmation Talk

> *Actions speak louder than words, but some of those actions are confusing without the words. Horacio Jones*

The Bond and the Title goes hand in hand. If I really want you, you will get the title and appropriate treatment and behavior from me. The Bond is between you and I. The title is a representation of the future plans that we have made with each other. No title means no future plans. The title is the name of our relationship. The title is our declaration to the world of our one on one love. The title represents the fact that our "other options" are completely cut the fuck off and irrelevant.

I'm personally a fan for the confirmation talk (titles). We are either together or not together. There is no in between with me. You are NOT my woman just because I treat you like it. You are my woman when I define WHY I'm treating you that way, while presenting plans for OUR future and adding a commitment with clarity When a man really sees you in his future he makes sure it is KNOWN with both actions AND words. If you have to wonder, then you are not his woman. That's why I say actions do not always speak louder than words, instead they go hand in hand. The title means nothing if the actions do not match. The actions are bullshit if the definition does not match.

A title (Confirmation talk or a defined answer to the "what are we" question) in my opinion, demonstrates a higher level of commitment. Confirming the status of the relationship with words AND actions is our declaration against the confusing "going with the flow" stage. Confirming the status of the relationship with words AND actions means that we are in a relationship together and we have plans for OUR future.

Our relationship title will never be "we know what we have" because no the hell we do not! Labeling you AND treating you as my girlfriend is the simple definition of our relationship and future plans. If I label you AND treat you as my friend, it means that we have a platonic bond. If I marry you, you become my wife. That means that I am ☐ percent sure that I am spending my life with you and there is NO ONE ELSE. Friends with benefits = friendship = booty calls.

All bonds and actions (treatment) must correlate accurately and consistently with the titles placed. If your bond is labeled as the following for 5 months or more, you're in a Situationship:

1. We're just chilling
2. Going with the flow
3. We know what we have
4. Nobody has to know
5. Low-key bae
6. I do not want a relationship

For each individual, the title has different meanings. Maybe you desire a title in order to feel secure and to know that your companion is willing to tell the world about you. Maybe you feel content knowing that they do not mind sharing that you exist. Even if they do not broadcast it, you'll be content just as long as they do not HIDE it. The title shows you that you are important and that they are not keeping their options open. It also clears up any uncertainty about the future and eliminates hesitation.

Some people want a title so that they do not have to read between the lines and make assumptions. Embarrassing assumptions occur when relationships aren't defined. So, titles define the bonds that you have with people. For example, not introducing her as your woman could lead her to believe that you are trying to hide the fact that she is your girlfriend, although maybe not deliberately. She will feel very secure if you make an effort to validate that she is very important and that the relationship has a plan for the future. This applies to women who hesitate to "claim" their men as well.

Are Titles Important?

Should the title really matter if you already have a strong bond? My answer = HELL YES.

When I say "title" I'm not talking about the words "boyfriend and girlfriend". I'm talking about that "confirmation talk." The confirmation talk is the discussion about defining the bond that you have with someone. The "talk" is about communicating and understanding if plans for a future together will be made. Those discussions could be private or public. But, that "what are we" talk is important to eliminate confusion.

The reason why people are confused, is because their emotions are official, but the title or relationship status is still TBA. Therefore, they are unsure as to whether or not, they should have their actions correspond more with the title of "we are single" or correspond to their emotions of "officially together".

Some people want the relationship title because it broadcasts their relationship publicly, letting everyone, including each other, know that they are taken. Titles show that you have serious plans for the future. Others are more into low-key, discrete relationships; resisting the title because it makes things public.

Half Single

Face it, no matter how many
times that you explain to them
that you do not want anything
serious, treating them like it is
more than what you say it is and
having sex with them will most
likely confuse them. Even though
you are single, they do not
consider you fully single. The
funny thing is, even though it is
not an official relationship, when
they start acting single or settle
down with someone ELSE, you
are going to feel like they
cheated on you. What the both of
you fail to realize is that there
was never a relationship
established...

#DearWomen

I want to dedicate this to the women. I see your tears even if they may not fall from your eyes. It is projected in your desire to find love & happiness, but always in the wrong places and in the hands of men that do not truly love you. I wish you could see yourselves for how I view all of you; lovely, beautiful, worthy of love. But you are steady striving for all of the wrong things with dating. You are slowly killing parts of who you are because of certain actions that you repeat just like other hurt women.

Your mind, body and soul should not come at a cheap price. So why invest in bootleg love? You are doing just that - selling yourself short. These men will come and go, but those demons you bury deep within, will hunt you until you break the cycle. After every heartbreak, those demons get stronger. You need to let go, let go of whatever it is you are holding onto and find something new, something within yourself that says "I do not just know that I deserve better, I'm going to do better". The thing is, if you continue down this route, it will never change; different men and same results.

Whatever bed you lay in, whatever lips you kiss, whatever hand you hold that does not bring you happiness or see you for you, is a disservice to yourself.
Sincerely Horacio

I Understand: Part 1

"You are in charge of your happiness. At this point, your tears from disappointment and heartbreak are no one's fault, but yours if you STAY. You keep entering these Situationships knowing what the outcomes may be, but ignoring them. Do you not love yourself enough to know what is best for you? If not, I'm here to tell you that YOU DO. You are worthy of love and respect. Keep telling yourself that until you believe it. Some people will only treat you the way that you allow them to. The more you continue with these Situationships, the bigger hole of depression you're digging for yourself."

<u>X   Horacio Jones</u>

Put Her In Her Place

At first, I did not understand what women meant by "put me in my place." I was dealing with very immature and petty women who WANTED to argue and cause drama. They were used to having to prove their worth and when I did not want to argue, they'd assumed that I did not care about them. But, I grew tired of the drama and instead felt like why the hell am I trying to tame these grown ass woman? Over time, I learned that "putting a woman in her place RESPECTFULLY" does wonders.

Women want to be put in their place RESPECTFULLY because it turns them on. A man who has the balls to correct them is a big turn on. They want a self-assured man and a leader. That is why they test us so much. They want to see if we have balls.

If you let her get away without correcting her RESPECTFULLY, then you go into the friend zone category. But, if you call her out on her bullshit without getting emotional, abusive or disrespectful about it, you go into a different category - the "I might marry him and fuck him like crazy" category.

A woman who is in control of her man is not comfortable because she knows it is not natural. She will seek out stronger men who challenge her. She will test men constantly until she finds what she is looking for; a man with balls, a real man who knows the ways of the world, and a man who will take control of the situation and tell her to calm the hell down. This is what she wants without having to tell him. Even men want to be put in their place. Most of us want to alternate between following and leading.

Dear Single Mothers

She said "my daughter does not have a father. I'm the father." What pisses her off the most is that he is "free". While she is tied up late night taking care of HIS child, he is out messing around with women who call him daddy. But, his child barely knows who her daddy is. While he is at the CLUB, she is putting the baby in the CRIB. While he is sipping on Cîroc bottles, she is sipping on baby bottles, making sure her child is getting enough to eat. She cannot count on him to lend a hand, but she can count on one hand, how many times he already has. 1. Xmas, 2. Father's day, 3. Birthday. 4. Late night booty calls while she is lonely because she does not have time to find a new man.

On top of that, she doesn't believe anyone would date her AND her child. She doesn't want HIM, she wants his HELP. But the only thing he wants to do is help her undress. His clothes are right back on before she can even ask *"are you keeping your child this weekend?"* It kills her how he only sticks around because he feels obligated. He never offers to spend time, unless it is for 15 seconds... long enough to post a video on Instagram, making it seem like he is always there.

Single mothers are dateable. Many of them are tough and independent. Many of them are already great mothers (weren't you looking for someone who would be a great mother?). They are patient, but have low tolerance for bullshit. Many of them do not play games, or have time to fool around. These women take their relationships seriously, and are willing to keep you around if the relationship is a good thing for both her and her child. Do not knock it before you try it.

Sometimes dating is unpromising. You never know who is really genuine about understanding your responsibilities as a mother, which are basically no days off. No free weekends or nights.

I like to admit my mistakes. My biggest one was allowing myself to become so busy trying to make something work and not wanting to let go, that I forgot that the point of being with someone was to accept them for who they really are and be happy with that. If I do not like who they really are, I should not try to force them to be compatible with me. Horacio Jones

Love

We know what makes us feel good, and we learn what makes other people feel good. What if the reason why we do not understand love the same way is because love doesn't always look the same way? Love comes out differently.

What if, love is masked by fear of being alone?

Who are we to tell them differently, if we cannot define love ourselves?

I want love to be the glue that holds us together through thick and thin, allowing us to forgive each other for mistakes, to compromise when necessary and putting the other person's needs before our own. Love should feel like complete happiness of loving yourself, and loving how you can love someone else.

There may be as many definitions of what love actually is as there are lovers to define the word. With our many different understandings of romance, passion, adoration, devotion, affection and courtship, there may not be a standard one size fits all definition of "love" as love is felt and expressed differently from each and every one of us. I think that with this business trying to define love actually drives it away instead of simply enjoying what it feels like.

Falling In Love

Our main drive is to expand ourselves as much as we can and to feel important. One of the ways we accomplish this is through our loving relationships with other people.

Have you ever wondered why you fell in love with specific people? Why THAT particular person? Why not someone else? I believe that we fall in love with certain people because we all have a check list of things that we want in a partner. A lot of the things on our lists may be subconscious, and of course, some are more important to us than others. We hold on to certain traits on those lists so much that we are willing to settle for less, just because that particular person fits important characteristics of our lists.

The conditions that a person must meet in order for us to love them varies. For example, some people fall harder for physical characteristics, such as race, skin tone, hair type, and body shape. While other people fall for the intangible characteristics such as the way a person sounds, the way they look at them, their work ethic etc. That's why we are capable of falling for imperfect people. We understand that no one will ever match every single trait.

Friend Zone

Someone who does not match the list, or at least some important characteristics of it, then becomes "ineligible" to be my partner, therefore ending up in the friend zone. The characteristics in your list are distinctive and specific to you depending on your, standards, experiences and principles.

Cannot Seem To Move On

Furthermore, this checklist theory is why we "cannot move on". Someone could fit our love criteria so well, that we feel as though no one else could be a better match. We lose sight of the millions of other people in the world and the probability of finding better matches, and that is why we never recover from breakups.

Self-Love

Do we love ourselves, or do we just love the thought or ideas we have? Do we fall in love with who we want to be, who we used to be, or with who we actually are? Are you in love with who we have potential to be, or who everyone else says we are?

I love myself. I think those who do not love themselves will find it difficult to love others fully. Loving yourself should be a completely natural thing, it lies in human nature to want to feel good about ourselves, even though we constantly battle opinions of others. Think about it; all of the good things you have going for yourself, all of the things you live for, the things you've done to help people, all of the things you can do or will do... aren't they all worth loving yourself for? It should feel wonderful to embrace yourself for everything you are and everything you have. You are unique. Embrace your rareness. Feel good about being the only you, and imagine what good you can do for everyone around you once you embrace yourself. You are a good person, no matter what anyone else says. Just look inside yourself and see it.

Benefits of Self Love:

1) You not only know your worth, but you will not settle for less, thinking someone else will change for you. The absence of their love does not mean you should throw away your individual identity. You do not NEED them to validate your love when you are full of it already.

2) You know what love feels like. You know how to love others. You can spot real love and distinguish between fake love.

3) You can give and receive love.

4) You are better prepared to re-adjust if your love was ever taken for granted. You've built yourself high enough to not be able to fall too far from being able to withstand and accept betrayal.

5) You'll be happier with giving the loved version of yourself to someone who desires the best version of you.

I swore to never force anyone to stay somewhere they did not want to be; not because I did not want them, but because I believed that true love is expressed in the form of freedom. It seemed very apparent to me that you knew I wanted to stay, but at the time I did not know how to forgive and forget, I questioned if that's even possible. I peacefully surrendered to the option of leaving because, at the time, I did not see any reasons to stay. I often wonder how much effort was required to stick it out. But on this journey to find the type of love I lost, I found out that I may or may not know a lot, but I know I loved you, I just could not have the honest version of you.

I Don't Deserve Shit

Deserve: [dih-zurv]: verb (used with object), deserved, deserving.

- To merit, be qualified for, or have a claim to (reward, assistance, punishment, etc.) because of actions, qualities, or situation:

My belief is that "I deserve better" in relationships usually means that there is a baseline for treatment and character. Being a good man or woman should be that baseline. That baseline suggests that people should be treated respectfully in any relationship. It suggests that everyone deserves natural human rights. It explains why we settle for less and still feel as though we deserve better. We believe that we deserve the "decent human behavior baseline" no matter who we are with and for however long we are with them. We see potential when we settle for less and it is not because we feel as though we deserve less. We just feel that over time of working on the relationship, we will get what we deserve; respectful and loving treatment (baseline).

Even with that being said, I'm so confused by people saying that they deserve things. The word 'deserve' is thrown around way too much these days. The word "deserve" just seems so vague to me nowadays and I am more enthusiastic about the word "desire" better because it implies that we really want something, but are not entitled to it just because we say that we want it. People use it so much that it has lost all meaning in my eyes. The word itself sounds exaggeratingly selfish when used in reference to relationships in a way in which I have never understood.

My question is, why do so many people believe that they "deserve" anything? Growing up in the south, I was always taught that it's not about what Socioeconomic status you grew up in, where you were born, or who your parents were that could get you what you "deserve." I was taught it's up to you to make something of

96

yourself because we aren't entitled to shit these days unless it's already yours.

Some people believe that just because someone is treating them like shit for months on end, that they DERSREVE better even when they choose to STAY. We've all been in a shitty relationship, but it was because of our choices that those relationships lasted as long as they did after giving a million chances. My belief is that we did not DESERVE anything other than what we were CHOSING to settle for. Saying that we deserve better is sometimes a way to feel good about ourselves without actually doing anything about it except playing the victims. In life, you get what you earn, not what you deserve.

What if we stopped searching for the relationships that we THINK we deserve? What if we learn how to focus internally and decide what kind of relationships we want and need, and then understand that they are not going to be perfect? If you want better for yourself, you have to put in the work in all aspects of your life. If you feel as though you deserve something, you should prove it to yourself by putting in the work and earning it. Yes, this means leaving people who give you less if you feel as though you deserve more.

The Truth Won't Always Set You Free

The truth will not set you free, but it will make you feel uncomfortable. If you are trying to deny it, reject it, or ignore it, the truth complicates things for you. Accepting the truth means that you have to get out of your comfort zone and face reality. But people do not appreciate reality when the perceptions of their fantasies are better.

The truth will force a lot of people to dislike you. The truth may not agree with what society says, so anyone going against it, would be considered hating, awkward or weird. If you are the truth, the people around you will be uncomfortable. No one wants you around. If anything, the real truth may scare away some of the "sleeping" people around you.

If the mass majority of people are always telling each other what they already agree with, accepting the opposite as the truth, may definitely be pointless to them. There's no need for the truth when a fantasy is way easier to accept than the reality that isn't desirable at all. You know that your truth isn't the truth that they want to accept. They hear the truth, but has it set them free?

No, because we find ways to differentiate our truth from other people's truth. The truth for one may not apply to another. What we should do is find our connection with our truths and see how we feel about them when we compare them. At the end of the day, whatever truths you choose to accept, you have to deal with the consequences. So speak the truths that allow you to feel good and be happy about not having to deny reality or paint different pictures. The truth may not set you free, but it will teach you how to be free if you are willing to accept it.

Emotionally Promiscuous

Be cautious of people who are "emotionally promiscuous." Emotional promiscuity is when a person constantly falls for every single person that they meet. Getting emotionally attached to everyone too soon is dangerous. This kind of wear and tear on your heart can be harmful to a person's emotional health, and definitely lead to sexual promiscuity. Feelings develop too easily for you, which leads to emotional cheating. You cannot be trusted because you like EVERYBODY.

Time Heals

Eventually you get up again and put
yourself out there (aka give a damn).
Being single is a great way to figure
out what you like and do not like.
Take the time to know who YOU are,
and what you can offer. Then you
can appreciate what a person has to
offer in return when you finally
decide to let love in again. Horacio
Jones

I Understand: Part 2

"It's not just about the choices this woman is making with men. It is about the fact that she hasn't learned the lesson yet. It doesn't matter that her best friends are the observers and givers of love during her hard times if she pushes them away every time they try to help. What matters is the lesson. If this woman is not tired of going through it, she will KEEP going through it until she gets completely fed up. This concept covers life in general.

We all see faults clearly when we are the observer of these women. Just because we see it doesn't mean that our solutions are the best for them. She may not even want help because she may not know she needs it, or be in a place mentally and emotionally where she is willing to be receptive to it. She has to get there on her own.
Just because we all see it, doesn't mean she will. The lesson is hers to learn, not yours to teach. That is life's job. Let her live. Don't give up on her."

X   Horacio
Jones

Potential

When we fall for their potential rather than the actual person, we make our relationship out to be more than what it really is. We fall in love with the "Idea of being in love", and we ignore all of the signs that tell us that this person is no good for us. Or, we are very aware of those signs, but try to look past them.

We try to convince ourselves that we are happy. But are we really happy? If so, happy with what: The idea or the reality? Hopefully, we know the difference because all fantasies come to an end. Sooner or later, we'll have to deal with the reality of the situation and the fact that the person we are with, is not really what we want or need.

Sometimes You Have To Accept The Fact That Certain People Will Never Go Back To The Way They "Used To Be." In Due Time, True Colors and Intentions Will Reveal Themselves. Maybe it is Not That They're Changing. Maybe You Are Just Starting To Realize Who They Really Are. Horacio Jones

... Maybe we cannot help but fantasize about the future; about "what could be." The future is unexplored territory with limitless possibilities and that is appealing to us. We have to remember to not forget that we are living in the PRESENT. We have to ask ourselves, "Is this current version of our lover worth the sacrifice of our time, effort, bodies, and love... Just to wait for their potential version to FINALLY arrive at our front door with everything that they SHOULD HAVE BEEN DOING in the first place.

What are they doing RIGHT NOW that influences our decision to "stick it out" until SOMEDAY arrives? We see certain potential, but they see a whole different version and maybe that is why a conflict exists. SOMEDAY, we have to stop seeing people for who we want them to be and see them for who they show themselves to be; Actions reveal all we need to know.

Why Do We Fall For Potential?

The reassurance of the future creates hope that one day life will be as they say, so we accept it simply because it is consistent behavior, and human beings respond well to consistency in all forms.

It is simple: We fall in love with the potential of what someone could be instead of seeing the person for who he/she really are. A lot of times, people come off how they want to be seen. You fall for that person and then they change. You cannot accept who they really are because you have already accepted who you thought they were.

Potential - LATENT qualities or abilities that MAY be developed and lead to future success or usefulness.

LATENT - existing but NOT YET developed or MANIFESTED; HIDDEN; CONCEALED.

So, it is a mistake to think that there is only one person who possesses those characteristics that YOU see in them, that aren't even apparent yet. If you are obsessed with the potential of a particular person, you have to ask yourself, "What's so great about this person's potential?"

Simple Shit

I do not want much. I just want the real
thing. I want someone who has a growing
crave and desire for me but doesn't
necessarily NEED me. I want someone who is
already full of love, not someone that I have
to complete. I want someone that wants me
to be better for US, not just for them.
Someone who is working on their own shit
and I come along and make life easier and
more enjoyable. I want somebody that'll give
and take without feeling obligated and isn't
keeping track of what they give because they
know I'm not playing games. Just be real. I'm
not even asking for much Horacio Jones

I want a give and take relationship without
feeling like I'm taking advantage of you. Or
without any of us feeling like we owe each
other. If you are carrying around a whole
bunch of shit in your bag — trust issues,
bitterness, exes — I just want you to know
that you do not need that when you are with
me. Let's not be bitter, let's both be better. I
want people to look at us and have to
wonder who the better half is because both
of us have our shit together or working to
get things together. This is possible. This is
simple shit.

Distance

Regardless of the physical distance, the emotional connection should be there. When that deep emotional connection is not established, or when trust issues take over, more "distance" is created. The extra distance between us makes some things "inaccessible."

Staying Committed; if there's no emotional bond, the distance doesn't mean anything, even if I lived across the street. We could physically be right in front of each other and not feel a damn thing anymore. If there ever comes a time when the anxiety associated with the emotional distance surpasses the enthusiasm to make things work, (causing us to not only feel physically deserted, but emotionally lonely as well) it may be because "stood" ...no longer "stands". What "stood" was a strong understanding and willingness to remain together no matter how far apart we were from each other.

Long distance relationships can work. The woman I loved the most had moved back to Colombia when we decided to be together. It worked because our love and desire to be happy with each other exceeded the nervousness of being apart for so long. I knew who I wanted. She knew who she wanted. That's all that mattered.

Some people will say it is a sign of weakness, to "Wait" to be with someone so far away. But that's not THEIR love story, it is OURS. To us, it is not a waste of time. It displays strength, courage and evidence that no time or distance can drift two people apart who are completely committed and in love with each other.

Make Long Distance Relationships Work

Set some ground rules and realistic expectations. We should have a GOAL. We'll need an app, like FaceTime, Skype, and even WhatsApp where we can dress up and go on cybernetic dates to make our distant relationship more exciting. Ultimately, we'll have a plan to actually be in person together someday, but understand why it cannot be at the MOMENT. Therefore, perseverance and patience are also imperative. Most importantly, we have to COMMUNICATE often in imaginative and creative ways. Someone who really wants you will do everything in their power to keep you close, because they recognize that any arrangement of distance yields doubt.

Emotionally Unavailable:

Being emotionally unavailable doesn't mean they cannot fall in love. It means that they are not serious about falling in love With US. They can be a good person and do everything right – but if they are not trying to open up emotionally, maybe we are wasting our time, although they will still be perfectly fine with receiving our attention and affection and of course sex. The lack of emotional connection is what ultimately eradicates the relationship.

The emotional distance generates problems because SOME of us think that we can determine why that other person is emotionally unavailable, then try to "fix" it or change them. Over time, it just becomes too stressful because our effort hasn't made them express deeper feelings. So, we either keep trying, break up with them, or cheat (emotionally before physically).

Physically Unavailable:

Being psychically unavailable to us doesn't mean that they are being physically available to someone else. Everyone doesn't show physical affection the same way. They do not want to cuddle and kiss all day. They value space. Stress from everyday life or experiences while growing up could effect that. It becomes a problem when we expect people to be just as affectionate as we are, even when it comes to sex. It is nothing that a little bit of communication cannot fix because all we want is their reassurance that they are attracted to us physically.

Mentally Unavailable:

This one is the most important because they cannot be available to us in any aspect (other than sex) if their mind isn't focused. If they cannot hold a conversation or grow intellectually simply because they are not on our level mentally, it should turn us off. Immature and petty people annoy me; it is like dating a little kid. These mentally unavailable people are most likely superficial and their mind is based on materialistic things, not on fulfilling our emotional desires? Dump them.

How To Move On

You'll lose yourself
Through the pain
Of not having the effort
And commitment reciprocated.
Nevertheless, through losing yourself,
You begin a process
Of finding yourself after chaos.

After chaos,

There's peace.

Then,

Balance....

Finally, you'll pick yourself UP....

That's the only direction we can
Take once we are strong enough
To walk away. - Horacio Jones

How to Move On
Part I: Face Reality

If I want to get over someone who I KNOW I should not be with, the first thing I have to do is face reality: THEY DO NOT WANT TO BE WITH ME. If they did, they'd be here right now, making things work. If we were such a great match, they would be in it as much as I am. If we were meant to be together, we would be together or at least working on it; not working away from it. I would not be on the receiving end of the lies and pain that'll only make it harder to trust THEM, even later down the road. That is backwards. I do not want to go that way.

When you love someone so much, you tend to have tunnel vision. The pain hits you out of nowhere and you are never really prepared to have to move on with your life all of a sudden. You cannot see your life functioning as it used to without them. All you want is to find a way to get them back. Even if they do not want it.

So, I FACE REALITY, accept it, heal my own damn heart as fast as possible. I cannot lie, it hurts. I do not want to fake like I'm all ok, trying to hide it or suppress it. Living in denial can feel good for a little while; we are allowed to feel like shit initially. We can be angry, sad or disappointed, whatever. But, one of the last things we should do is run from it because it'll eat us up inside. FACE IT.

I moved on when I
realized that I did
not have to stop
loving them. I just
had to start loving
myself more.

– Horacio Jones

I honestly think it is better to go through this pain now than to postpone it for later and live in false hope, thinking they'll want us back. Even when it is obvious that they are still doing the same shit that they were doing to us, to someone else, we STILL run back after suppressing the reality.

Suppressing the pain will only prolong my recovery, not make it go away. The person who would rather do that "us" thing with someone else, has a mind of their own, and we cannot change it by force. We cannot even persuade them by "showing them our worth." They have free will and unless they choose us, we'll have to walk away. As simple as that. Easier said than done though.

Easier Said Than Done

You have to be sick and tired of hurting – fed ALL the way up – and willing to move on AND CUT THEM OFF. No more saying that "It is easier said than done". Is it really easier said than done? We SOMETIMES talk a lot of shit, but we do not do half of the things we say we were going to do. It is much easier to tell yourself that you are going to end the bullshit ass relationship that you put so much effort into, than it is to actually leave and stay away.

If we are going to say it, the first thing we must do is not go back on our word with every other thing in our lives, as practice. For example, if we are going to go to the gym, let's make proper life adjustments in order to make time for the gym. That does not have to be said. Just do it. I know you cannot buy the house or car right now, but let's make the proper life adjustment today that'll set us on the path. Just do it. I know it is so hard to break up. There is a long road to recovery. So, why postpone it by staying with someone who's wasting your time? You do not have to say anything anymore, just start doing things. Get excited about what you do, not what you say.

How to Move on
Part II

When you continue to be with
someone who you know is no
good for you, you are deciding to
be on the receiving end of
whatever bullshit that they throw
at you. Sometimes "staying" =
allowing them to hurt you and
take control of your love life.
Haven't you had enough?

After you face reality, change your
mindset then raise your
standards. Accept that the pain
will last for a while. Change what
you demand of yourself. NEVER
forget how much it hurt when you
had them. 9 times out of 10, all
they have earned from you is
forgiveness and front row seats to
your recovery... without them.

Moving On Steps

1. Face reality
2. Don't say… just do.
3. Do not ignore it, deal with it.
4. Meditation or prayer.
5. Hang around your friends and family more. People usually distance themselves from people who are telling them to LEAVE.
6. No more EXCUSES — stop defending them. Do not keep making excuses for them. It is never a good enough reason for them to lie to you and cheat. It is not YOUR fault.
7. Stop inventing reason to contact them.
8. Start focusing on just YOU – You've allowed yourself to become consumed with making things better with this person. Instead of putting YOURSELF first, you've been putting THEM first. And you've made them your only source of happiness. Go do some things that make YOU happy because your ex won't. Spend time with yourself and NO TIME WITH THEM.
9. Workout. Burn off steam. Get sexy. Concentrate on your health, you'll feel a lot better by taking care of yourself. Once you see the results, you will realize that you are the person that you want to fall in love with.
10. Say no - they're used to getting their way. No more SEX!!! You'll really see their true colors. Sex will have you going back on your word. Can we hang out? No! Do you miss me? No response. Netflix and Chill? No!
11. Do not sit around thinking you miss them. What you miss is the person you wanted them to be and who you thought they were. You were happy before them, you will be happy after them.
12. CHANGE YOUR MINDSET. "I desire a better person, not a better THEM because that version doesn't exist."
13. No guilt. Do not feel bad about leaving. Delete their number, pictures off your social media. NO MORE CONTACT. Leave them alone so you can heal and figure YOURSELF out. Stay off their profiles! They'll tell you how "sorry" they are and how "depressed" they are because they do not have you. Guilt is a dangerously

powerful emotion. And they WILL use it against you.

14. No "let's just be friends" arrangements. Do not play yourself. Feelings are still there. Stay away. No checking in. Do not fool yourself into believing your situation is different, because unfortunately, most of these situations are the same. You cannot move on while being friends. YOU ARE IN LOVE WITH THEM.

15. Be proud that you finally put yourself first. Get your shit together. I'm just saying, you can do better.

Why is it hard?

Time and distance. That's all we need to move on, right? Then why is it that after months and even years, we still feel the pain? What if it is not even about them? Maybe, it is because we cannot move on from ourselves and memories, not the actual people who hurt us? Because, we are stuck on what we should have done differently, what we should have known, what we should have seen, what we should have been.

After space and time away, we still hate thinking about it. If only I hadn't been like this, If only I had done that. It is The Situationship Cycle, where we only blame ourselves.

We start blaming ourselves over time, because the pain becomes romanticized. Meaning, the anger towards them fades, and we remember most of what was good with them. But, we also remember more about what's "wrong" with us. Underneath whoever we are struggling to let go of, lies the reality that this is so much about how we feel about ourselves and what memories make us feel.

The memory of them is what makes it hard. When someone we love leaves, they take with them the physical pieces of the relationship. They cannot take away the emotions, the thoughts and the memories. These feelings eventually scatter. After that chaos, new, more intense feelings take their place: Pain and anger towards the memory of the person who left.

Most of us try to forget these memories, which usually leads to more displaced frustration. We try to distract ourselves from these memories by using other people. Although, it may provide a temporary "pardon" from the pain, we tend to also develop deep emotions for those temporary people as well. Nevertheless, you'll eventually encounter those memories again as soon as you are by yourself and vulnerable. You will be juggling the pain from your ex and this new emotional attachment. The only cure is to accept those memories, not run from them or to someone else. Accepting the memories as lessons takes time, but time is a healer.

Even with
the memories,
life
goes on.
Your break
up won't
stop anything,
unless you
allow it. You should
embrace
the memory instead
of trying to suppress it.

Your Ex can still be a friend...

It's rare to find someone who really, truly knows you and still loves you, who will always be on your side and will always look out for you.

The essence of life is the connections that we make.

Why would I ever discard a relationship like that just because we were unable to stay together?

There isn't any sneakiness here; these are women that used to mean the world to me, a long time ago, and they're women who I like and appreciate, and that I get along well with. If that hadn't been the case we would've never been a couple in the first place.

The romantic bonding may have not worked out, but... we still care about each other in such a way that doesn't threaten our other relationships and friendships.

I actually find it sad when people who used to love each other end up treating each other like enemies. There's no reason you need to be enemies just because the romantic relationship didn't end up lasting for life.

Some relationships may be so toxic that they have to truly end. In my experience, those are rare exceptions.

Some People Force
You To Cut Them Off...

Sometimes, it's completely necessary to
cuff off, delete and block someone that has
become toxic and destructive. The secret is
this: you know that lack of physical contact
will kill any relationship. Use that to your
advantage. If you don't physically connect
after giving it an honest try to work things
out, your toxic relationship will suffer and
eventually die. Therefore, if you want to cut
someone off, you simply stop physically
dealing with the person after you've tried to
resolve the issues. The instant that you stop
messing around, the toxic relationship is over.
Then, you're left with the emotions and
memories. Which are way easier to deal with if
your ex isn't back in your bed...

why do people change after sex?

Most people who hook up with someone they really like wants to keep hooking up and chilling with each other as long as they can. But, things change drastically once feelings get involved if they let the feelings get the best of them. Once they allow their feelings to constantly over power their logic, the dynamics of the relationship changes. One person starts having sex and become increasingly clingy and needy, which may annoy the hell out of the other person. This is why people treat feelings like they are STDs; afraid to catch them and terrified to admit to having them. They "hide" their feelings so that they won't scare the other person away.

But, what ends up happening is that those feelings eat at them and eventually come out anyways. But instead of manifesting in the form of love and affection, it comes out as passive aggressiveness and pettiness when those feelings aren't reciprocated. The resentment is usually due to something involving increased demands and expectations that makes the other person cut things off after sex is involved. It doesn't make sense for most people to put in the time and effort to get with you sexually just to cut it off out the blue. So, for them to do it, there is usually a logical reason behind it. Most "quick feelings catchers'" behavior becomes more bothersome after sex is introduced into the situation. All the extra stuff they tend to do Is typically what makes the other person lose interest and cut things off.

They don't cut you off just because you caught feelings, they break things off when the behavior dramatically chances based on feelings and expectations.

On the other hand, like I mentioned before, some people are wolves in sheep's clothing. They think of sexual partners as prizes. They would do anything to have you and once they get to have sex, they lose interest because they got what they wanted and started chasing someone new. After sex, they quickly switch things up before you get too attached. They act a certain way to get what they want and when you give it to them, they see no point to keep the act up. That is when you really get to see what type of person they are, <u>after</u> you have slept with them. That's when the true colors come out.

119

Their goal is to simply have sex, and your post-sex behavior may be a turn off to them. Often times after sex, one person wants to start having conversations about expectations of love, relationships and commitment, and over time start essentially giving ultimatums. Or they start cursing you out because you haven't taken action to "make it official" and still haven't discussed "the next step" with them.

When someone is in it just for the sex and chilling, they see it as going from cool as fuck to annoying as fuck in less than a few weeks.

In conclusion,

It's certain changes in behavior that push us away. It seems like as soon as we have sex, we get the we "what are we" talk when we probably already told you that sex isn't going to change our mind about being in a relationship with you.

It's so easy to assume that we are the ones who change significantly after sex, but sex changes women also. They typically become emotionally attached after a sexual encounter. Especially if they're really feeling a guy, the sex was good, and he seems to be very into her as well.

That expectation that I'm supposed to change everything I've ever told her JUST because we had sex is unfair. Some women really believe that their sex is like Kryptonite for us.

Relationship Conformity

I feel that another reason why women change is because society tells them that they are of less value if they sleep with a man without a commitment. Those insecurities may make them want to push that man to be committed, even if one or both parties aren't ready/willing to be in a relationship. The way a man values a woman doesn't always change after sex but the way a woman values herself often does. Therefore, you see her insecurities reflected in her behavior.

From a guy's point of view, women need to understand that the collective opinion of society as it pertains to her individual behaviors without being committed to a man is relatively unimportant. She should relax and realize that while many people in society may be willing to push a standard, she and the man she's interested in aren't required to do the same.

She doesn't have to act on that pressure with desperation, trying to make him commit when he says he doesn't want to. What's wrong with a civil conversation before or after the sex? What's wrong with not acting on it at all at the moment?

Be your own person and free yourself from societal constraints that have no power over you. We all need to know ourselves well enough to recognize the change in our behavior and then be able to understand why WE have changed, men and women both. We should deal with how WE value ourselves and the pressures we give into from society.

Being self-aware is the most important thing for anyone. If we are self-aware then we know when we can bend societal rules for our benefit and when we cannot.

If you explain to the other person the reason why you changed, it may help them understand where you are coming from.

Lack Of Consistency.

Actions do not always speak louder than words because you can definitely misread actions. Ex: more dates, more time spent, more sex, more gifts are SOMETIMES signs of progress towards a real relationship to one person. While to the other person, those are merely signs of growing attraction and comfort, but they still don't want a relationship.

They will literally tell you over and over in many ways that they do not want a relationship even when the actions from your perspective show otherwise. Especially after meeting friends and family, or when the person gets jealous when you "talk" to someone else. You think, "they MUST want to be with me now because they are getting jealous." But Nah. They never said that they wanted you in the way that YOU want to be wanted. They literally said the opposite of that, but you are so focused on the actions alone because they make you feel good.

When you ignore the words and misread the actions, you'll feel like you were purposely misled and manipulated, lied too and used because what they said, what they did, and what you thought didn't match up. We are so used to more sex, more gifts, more dates and meeting family and friends, all indicating that the person wants to be with us in an official relationship. But, I've realized that we can be very wrong in the way that we perceive things.

Those aren't always signs that someone wants to be with us, but they are signs that someone is interested in us. Someone can very well have an intense interest in you, but not have that same desire for a relationship with you. Therefore, if we can't depend on actions that are apparently supposed to speak louder, what do we depend on to let us know if someone wants to be with us or not?

Consistency reveals intentions, which reveals how much you really want someone. And it also builds trust.

True Intentions: Consistency between actions and words!!!! They go hand in hand. How can we accept one without the other? No one should trust inconsistent people so why choose one over the other; actions over words? Because the words don't make you feel as good as the actions do?

To sum it up, actions and words being consistent is what speaks loudly. Consistency between words and actions reveal motives and true intentions. People are more likely to be inconsistent with things that they don't really want to say and do. People are more likely to be consistent with things that they really want to say and do. So you can't sit there and only look at someone's actions or only listen to the words. They have to go together to paint the whole picture. Don't stop listening to the words just because the actions make you feel good. And don't just listen to the words if the actions don't match. When you are consistent, you don't have to worry about people misreading you.

Nowadays,
you either
mislead people
or misread people.

"Next Big Thing"

We hate starting over. However, being afraid of opening up again DOES NOT mean that there is something WRONG with YOU. It has become a norm to stay to ourselves and deal with an ex just for familiar sex. But at some point, if you truly want a good relationship, better job, new car, new hobbies, health etc., you have to get ready to take a risk by stepping out again. Nevertheless, do not look down on yourself if you are afraid; everyone is afraid of change.

Date someone else. Do something else.

I do not think that people realize how important the NEXT person, place, or thing, is after rebuilding yourself. After a long while of "doing you," you'll still feel a little pain from your past, but there comes a time when you fully accept what's done is done. You forgave them. You do not hate them. You do not want them back. Although the love remains, you realized that it is ok to love people, but not have to be with them.

My goal is to love, not hate. I believe that forgiveness and acceptance are forms of love. You sometimes second guess if you are truly over the past relationship because there's still a void to be filled. You've done everything needed to move on... except one thing. START DATING NEW PEOPLE. That's mainly because you do not FEEL ready. The thing about that is, you'll only know that you are ready, once you try the dating scene again.

I will not act like it is a bad thing to fall in love again because the last phase of moving on, is dating someone new; creating better memories. The next big thing doesn't have to be a "person". You can go after that new job you want. You can buy that car. Go back to school Etc. You are ready to accept that "next big thing":

1. When you reestablish yourself as an individual.
2. Accepted that it is NOT only your fault.
3. You do not get angry about the past bullshit anymore.
4. When you STOP checking up on your exes and stop responding to them.
5. Happy on your own "Doing You".
6. Can have fun when you go out.
7. When you are emotionally available to invest in someone, or something else.
8. Dealt with your trust issues.
9. Ready to not let that random "pop up" by your ex stop you or draw you back in.
10. You are ready when you finally try.
11. When you finally stop worrying about if your ex is ever going to talk to you again after you have sex with someone else.

Getting Back With Your Ex

We obviously had feelings for each other before, so why not now? What we both need to do is think about the things that caused us to break up. We should examine these individually and decide if there are things that can be worked out between us. If we feel this way, then let's talk to one another about the issues we had. Let's communicate with each other, not argue. If we ever end up back together, then our relationship will be different, but it will also be much stronger.

Letting Go

Too often we get caught up in trying to obliterate people from our lives and memories when in fact, we should embrace every person in our lives for different reasons. We should appreciate everyone we meet because they are blessings, and all relationships with them teach us lessons. Our lives are collections of moments and blessings that remind us of how things used to be and motivate us to make better life choices. Simply put, the people we meet teach us how to treat ourselves.

I think that some of the pain of having to let go is dealing with the changes and adjusting to new, uncomfortable situations. The truth is, we eventually hurt less, but won't ever forget these people. Those memories are not a bad thing because every person we meet provide us with memories that teach us about life and ourselves by bringing out things in us, that we never knew existed. It is not a bad thing to let go.

Netflix and Chill

I love watching Netflix. It doesn't always have the best movies, but if you search through it for at least two hours straight, you might find something worth being addicted to. Most of the time, I watch Netflix alone and order pizza all for myself. But I can't deny how fun it could be while watching Netflix with someone I really like.

I honestly don't like going out all of the time anyways. Sometimes, I just want to chill and honestly watch Netflix. But lately, everyone around the world has been shading having sex after watching Netflix as If It's something that has to happen or always happens. Or that if a guy asks a woman to watch Netflix, she now thinks he's not trying to put any effort into actually getting to know her.

Honesty: of course I WILL think about having sex. But that doesn't mean that THATS why I asked to "#NetflixAndChill". There's a 97% chance that I was going to watch Netflix even if you weren't there. So don't feel too special. But I realized that I will never again be able to say "want to watch Netflix and chill?" without a woman thinking it's really about sex instead of actually watching a movie...

Not every Netflix movie session Is a netfuck! I won't sit here and lie by telling you that I won't be thinking about sex while watching Netflix. Sex will be on my mind. But that doesn't mean we have to have sex. It doesn't mean I'm going to reach over and strip you naked without your consent and it definitely doesn't mean that I'm automatically using Netflix to trick you into having sex with me. Especially if we're still getting to know each other. Remember, it takes TWO to have consensual sex. So you can't sit here and blame a man when you also wanted to have sex. If you want to blame anything or anyone, don't blame Netflix, don't blame the guy, don't blame the girl, blame it on our self-control. This might blow your mind, but you can actually choose not to have sex during, before, or after watching Netflix. Netflix foreplay is optional. Crazy right? I knowwwwww.

One thing people seem to constantly forget about watching Netflix and chilling is their lack of self-control. You can't blame the person who asked you to watch Netflix. You can't blame Netflix. You wanted to have sex too!!! So, when someone wants to watch Netflix and chill, they WILL think about having sex with you. Is it THAT bad to think about? You don't HAVE to have sex. It's a choice. Self-control is the main protection you need when watching Netflix.

There's a lot of women out there spoiling men with Netflix sex. Time and energy are the biggest investments someone can make to show that it's real. So, go out sometimes too.

I honestly prefer Netflix over going out. We can set a table. Eat. Drink wine. Then pull out the couch. Turn on the flat screen and watch whatever... Or turn on Hulu.... Or go to letmewatchthis.com to watch HD bootlegs, order pizza, Dunkin' Donuts... If we have sex... It's not because of Netflix... It's because we CHOSE to have sex. Netflix dates can be inexpensive and fun when the intentions are pure. Just make sure watching Netflix and chilling isn't all you do when dating someone because 9 times out of 10, they are going to think it is already a wrap; once someone knows you're a "Netflix And Chill" guy or girl, they'll have you coming over all the time, chilling all the time but still no real dates.

In conclusion, getting Netfucked isn't new at all. We haven't really seen much evolution from, "want to come over and watch a movie?" in the 90s. In the 2000s, it's "Netflix and Chill." Way faster than sticking DVDs into a machine hoping that it doesn't have any scratches on it. So, Netflix isn't the issue at all. It's the schemes and plans that make things go wrong. By go wrong, I mean, someone actually wants to watch something but ends up with penis in their mouth and now that's the only routine for months.

Now, it's ok to have that in your mouth. Because you wanted it there. It wasn't forced. Oral sex is dope. But months later, you STILL haven't done anything other than text, chill and fuck... That's NOT Netflix's fault.

If you are open-minded, mature, and have self-control... Watching Netflix with someone isn't a problem as long as it's not all you do each time you see each other. Go out on outdates sometimes. Museum and chill. Dinner and chill. Homework and chill. Club and chill. It is not a problem when you know that you can control yourself. You might even fall in love and have Netflix to thank for all of it, right?

If you want to watch Netflix with someone, go watch Netflix with them. If you don't want to have sex during and after Netflix, don't. We are adults □. No one tricks you into a #netfuck. You CHOOSE to have sex. Self-control....

Love Your Selfie

Social Media Fuels Insecurity

Social media gives us the ability to cut, edit and paste pictures, videos and quotes that we choose to show. This helps develops a false self that is usually with "less flaws" than the actual self.

You can basically be whoever you want to be on social media. You can be a model, photographer, writer, rapper, baller, comedian, love guru, relationship expert, the possibilities are endless. You could catfish people and make up a whole new person and pretend to be that person. You can grow your fan-base by cropping out other people's faces and names, then by claiming all of their artistic work and promoting it all as yours. You can accomplish creating a fake version of yourself by posting certain things, and omitting others.

And this is how the users of social media promotes a world where everyone has less imperfections, breeding jealousy and placing all of the importance on image alone.

Whenever people begin to obsess over their image, they become more insecure and often disappointed with parts of who they REALLY are and what they REALLY do after hiding it, rather than dealing with it.

Don't Be jealous

People who appear to be living these lively and luxurious lives and having so much fun doing it makes others feel inferior.

There were nights where I laid in bed wondering if I was living the full potential of my life. I would look at those images in question if whether or not I needed to start going out and doing more because I was missing out or not doing the things others were posting about; like going on vacations, partying and shopping.

I felt insecure because I started thinking that I was not as "liked" as everyone else. I was constantly comparing the amount of likes and followers…. trying to keep up with them. I constantly obsessed over getting more followers and likes. I wanted people to think "Wow, he is the best writer. I want to follow him". I was a bit obsessed over how people perceive my quotes. And it put me on a path of self-destruction.

I became jealous, and upset. Scrolling through my feed and seeing that other people are out with friends while was at home doing nothing. Comparing my life to others caused me to believe that EVERYONE was living better than me.

The lesson learned: Never look at others to witness the gold you hold inside yourself. And if people seem to be gaining more favorable circumstances, instead of feeling down on yourself, practice being happy for others. It will be hard at first, but when you cultivate true happiness for the success of others, happiness follows you.

Conclusion

Social media is a place of constant comparison. Every time someone scrolls down their timeline, they see pictures of someone else's apparently perfect life. They are shown the blessings of someone else's life, and ignore the blessings of their own.

Comparing your life to someone else is dangerous because it leads to thoughts of feeling like you're not enough.

Depression comes from within, not social media. It is more important for people to love their own lives, and be content with themselves.

⁉
Stop Social Media Recklessness

1. No Over-Sharing About Your Relationship.
2. No Indirect subliminal post (Petty Posts).
3. No Keeping in Touch with Your Ex who is disrespectful to your relationship with someone else.
4. No Flirting in the comments and dm when it clearly makes "bae" feel uncomfortable.
5. No Blocking each other just to LOOK single.
6. No Having dating apps when you are already in a relationship.

If stopping all of this reckless social media behavior is asking for too much from you, don't be in a fucking relationship then. But of course most of us will find out about the "I don't want a relationship loophole" where you can still get all of the benefits of a relationship but, no one can complain about your single people type behavior on social media because technically you are "single." I will keep repeating this.

Here, these rules MIGHT make sure the use of social media doesn't sabotage your "Bae status":

Rule #1: don't post like you're officially "babe" if you're not really "babe". The worst thing these days is becoming "Instagram official" before you're actually official. Then having to delete the pics. You need to have that conversation before you start prematurely broadcasting it.

Rule #2: Stop mindlessly scrolling: wasting time scrolling leads to sneaking a peak at exes and other bullshit. It's annoying to be with someone who is scrolling all day and snap chatting everything. Do you have to share EVERYTHING with the world? No. You don't need to check your notification and "like" every 5 minutes.

Rule #3: Log the hell off when you're upset. Jesus Christ! If you just had a fight, step away from the computer or your phone and don't bash your relationship to the world. All you're going to do is post shit that's going to make you feel bad about your relationship—or worse.

Rule #4: no flirty ass Friends or exes.

Social Media Relations

Post Me

Most people feel as though social media outlets are more fun when you can post photos and videos of that special someone who you enjoy spending time with. You want to show off babe. "His and her's" pictures. "Baecations". If there is a moment with babe, you're trying to capture it on snapchat, Instagram, Facebook, Tumblr, and whatever else out there. You just can't wait to share. I get it, this is the generation that we live in, so we can't sit here and pretend that social media isn't a big part of our relationships now.

A lot of these relationships actually started on social media. Maybe you were leaving a couple emojis under someone's picture. You sent the DM, the next thing you know, you're together. And now, you want to post together to SHOW all of the irrelevant people. A lot of the posts are genuine displays of love and affection. But another portion of those posts with babe are all about making sure everyone knows who you're with. Who's taken. Who's off the market. And when you find yourself doing all of the posting, but they barely share anything with or about you at all, you start to assume that they're trying to hide you.

I honestly cannot tell you how many times someone has sent me an email about not being posted on their lover's social media pages enough. They always assume that their relationship is being hidden. My thing is this, you can't really hide a relationship in which people who actually matter knows of its existence. Just because you don't post it, doesn't mean it is hidden. You know it exist, your friends and family know that it exists, babe knows that it exists and their families as well. So what difference does it make? Does sharing you on their page make your relationship more "together"? NO. What if your pages got deleted for some reason? Does that make you look too single or something?

I know that it's cool to see people like the photos or comment with words like "relationship goals" and heart-eye emojis on those shared pics with "babe", but just don't let those things make you believe in your relationship more than you already do offline. "Likes" from others don't strengthen you or your relationship.

Relationship Over-sharers

Everyone knows a relationship over-sharer: That person who constantly posts lovey-dovey shit about how blessed they are, shares exaggerated #WCW / #MCM photos and repeatedly announces their love to the world (or newsfeeds). But what do you know... Turns out, all of those posts could actually shed some light on their REAL relationship status.

You can look online right now and find the countless studies about people's posting behaviors. Most of those studies have found that couples who are content with their relationships are more likely to use social media to share affectionate posts, generally flouting their love.... but those posts are genuinely FOR EACH OTHER regardless of who is following their pages. But, the studies have also found that people with low self-esteem — that depends on how well their relationship is going — also post oversentimental pics... but they do it just to over show others, their partners, and mostly themselves that their relationship is still on and poppin'. They post more about what they WANT the relationship to LOOK like to compensate for the fact that the reality of the relationship is nothing like its virtual representation.

The difference between happy couples and those who over share to keep their self-esteem in check is that the self-esteem posters tend to brag about their relationship to others (as opposed to just sharing photos and writing sweet comments genuinely for each other), and then stalk their boyfriend or girlfriend's pages.

It's not only about the positive post about relationships. We can't forget about the arguments that are broadcasted all over social media. I don't know why people do it, but they love to share the whole argument in the form of screenshots of text messages or memes just to get back together and delete all of the bullshit that they posted the previous day. WHY?

#YourInstagramALiar

We all know those few people who lie about everything on social media. It's sad, yes, but is obvious. One important thing to remember about social media is that people put their best post forward, not their real post forward. Real problems, insecurity, or conflicts tend to be concealed and minimized as much as possible by these people. And if you think about it, there's not much wrong with hiding your real personal issues. We shouldn't expect people to broadcast the bad shit that's going on in their lives anyways.

But, if you feel like you have to lie or fake it until you make it by posting your relationship in a positive light knowing damn well that's not the real state, if you feel like you have to lie or fake it until you make it by posting your fake car, fake body, fake face…. when I say "fake", I mean by using someone else's pics to catfish your followers…. maybe you need to figure out how to actually work on your relationship and self so that it all progresses into the image you're painting for others. Lying to us doesn't fix the problems. In fact, why are you so concerned with what other people think about you and your relationship? Maybe this is centered around some type of depression with social media and self-esteem.

Happiness is not something you need other people to give you.

It is not hard at all to be happy. Choosing happiness is choosing to actively accept and understand people without being dependent on their actions or inactions. If we are waiting for someone to pop up, waiting to get a new job, waiting to graduate, waiting to buy a car, waiting for the pizza delivery man or for our friend's Netflix password, to be happy, we are *wasting* time. Finding happiness is supposed to be our own responsibility. Blaming other people for the lack of serenity in life will not bring much peace, but more frustration instead. Make yourself happy. How? What does happiness feel like?

Happiness is a rush. It is also a slow burn. It comes on all at once but it also builds up, like a pot of boiling with intense suspense. Everything forms to one point. You might not see the phases that are slowly working together to make you happy, but they're definitely there. Happiness is adrenaline-charged and delightful and unlike anything else, which is what makes it so hard to describe or understand. When you feel happy, that's all there is. There's good stress and good anxiety. There's no worry. There's no concern for something else that might be happening at the same time. Happiness takes control of everything else. It is a powerful emotion.

Happiness is when you've lived each day to the best of your inherent abilities and did all the things that you set out to do, and when you can live out another day feeling refreshed, rejuvenated, and without regrets.

Happiness is a very subjective thing. What makes you happy may not make me happy. It is all about what you want. If you want something and if you get it, you feel good. This feeling is happiness or satisfaction. But what you have may not give any happiness to me because I may not value it. The "thing" that you want could be psychological or material: It brings Joy. However, material things do not last, this means that you'll have to constantly replace them in order to be "happy."

You will never be happy
if you continue to
only search
for others to MAKE
you happy

25 Things to Do Every Day to Be Happy

1. Be optimistic
2. Stretch in the morning.
3. Think about things that you are happy about for a few minutes out of your day.
4. Step outside.
5. Laugh
6. Exercise
7. Express gratitude
8. Meditate
9. Say "thank you"
10. Make your bed, to clear your head. A messy bed is a reflection of your life.
11. Making the choice to eat better is making the choice to feel better.
12. Challenge yourself.
13. Touch someone
14. When you take something out, put it back when you're finished with it.
15. Read your mail, your text messages and email.
16. Listen to music for the mood that you want to be in, instead of the mood that you are currently in.
17. Give someone an honest compliment.
18. Putting your alarm across the room.
19. Say "hi" to your neighbors.
20. Prepare breakfast, snacks, or lunches to take with you throughout the week.
21. Clean your counters and dishes right when you are done with them instead of letting them pile up.
22. Acknowledge your parents and find out what they're up to today/let them know that you love them.
23. Writing down the things you need to do.
24. Tell a friend you love them.
25. Get enough sleep. Being tired makes it harder to be happy.

Before you say there's no good
men, just make sure you're a
good woman. Sometimes you
attract the lifestyle you live.
And the life you're trying to
live may be blocking blessing
because you haven't learned
your lessons. Good men deserve
better than women who aren't
trying to be better
Good men are everywhere,
but it depends on how you
look at them.

A good person to you, may not be good enough to another and so on. So you have to define what a good man is too YOU personally.

In general, good men focus on personal growth and inner peace. Therefore, you would have to connect at a more open minded, HEALED, vulnerable and emotional level rather than just physical a one. Not many "good guys" want to risk their inner peace by dating resentful and jaded women with disastrous dating habits and history. Good men avoid women who always says "I'm broken, I'm damaged, my exes are crazy."

When you heal the parts of you that your ex scarred, you'll start "seeing" where the good men are. Until then, you will keep dating the same type of men. If you keep having to "prove your worth," or "make him SEE" or "make him better" then you've just discovered your "type". You like men who you have to "convince", "change" or "manipulate" because the guys who already want you, already like you, already putting in effort aren't giving you the "challenge" of "proving your worth" so there's "no spark." You can't keep falling for the "they all seem good at first" stage because there are always signs.

The life you're living - if you're a club hopper, you may be running into the same type of men because men don't go to clubs looking for girlfriends and wives. We don't go there to dance and get to know you. We don't go there to be friends first. We don't go to parties to fall in love. If you're the "turn up turn up turn up" type, just know that the "turn up x3" guys aren't looking for relationships.

A man's usual "turn up x3" is balling with his homies, and having sex with multiple girls. It's time to turn the hell down.

Next, if you are always promoting how much you don't need a man, maybe that is blocking blessings because most men don't respond well to that. It is attractive to us to be an independent woman, but not a "fuck men" type. Just how you probably stay away from men who say "money over women." Those men repel good women. There are ways for men and women to make it clear what they "don't need" without sounding jaded

Relationship and Situationship Hoppers - How many women do you know that can actually stay single for any length of time? When I say "single" I mean REALLY single. I mean no secret fuck buddy sessions with an ex or low key new guy. I mean NOT waiting for the ex to come back. I mean NOT being a secret side chick. REAL SINGLE. Not dating 3 guys and texting one all day. Not one who is unwilling to break up with one guy unless another one is waiting on her bench to immediately take his place. Good men don't want the half single girl who always complain about "I don't know why my ex is always trying to talk to me, he's crazy." If you are a good woman:

A good man will find you.
You will find a good man.
The universe gives you what you put out.

why do we fall out of love?

when we first start dating, we do all kinds of things to impress, show respect and affection for each other. We don't get mad about things we normally would, and we generally work at the relationship as a team and have a higher level of tolerance to things that would typically drive us crazy.

this is because we haven't yet reached the point where we feel comfortable showing our "real" selves.

nevertheless, as time passes, a great deal of this "hiding true self" goes away. We start revealing who we really are and the tolerance declines. soon, people begin feeling comfortable and develop a minor sense of complacency.

"I know you and you're not going anywhere. I don't have to try as hard."

we start off showing affection and investing in getting to know and winning each other over. and it gradually decay as we get comfortable.

"I already got you."

fast-forward months or years later, and several things are regularly in place:

taking each other for granted.
we get lazy and stop trying to impress each other.
sex is no longer new and exciting, so we make love less...
more chilling, less effort to plan dates and surprises.
arguments over petty things and too fed up to work it out.

at the same time, we are treating the rest of the world like "I don't know you well enough to bullshit you," and as a result, we bring home all of the bullshit that we hold back throughout the day and throw all of the frustration onto each other. Instead of taking it out on others, we throw shade on each other thinking:

"I know you're not going anywhere. And if you don't listen to me nag, you obviously don't care about me."

that's bullshit.

in addition, we become increasingly more open to sharing what we really do and don't like about each other, which in turn, leads to arguments and hurt feelings, which leads to pettiness, passive aggressiveness, distance and more resentment.

consequently, what happens is that this increasing level of bullshit becomes an everyday routine and takes over. This makes day-to-day life with this person seem dull, repetitive and taxing.

and the next thing you know, we're both wondering what we saw in each other in the first place; "maybe it's time to find someone else more compatible"; we start seeking the excitement of new love to replace the old love.

and that's how relationships fall apart.

Feed Your Relationship

It is said that we are what we eat. I truly believe that every relationship has its own unique diet. Therefore, if we eat bullshit, we are bullshit; we have a horrible relationship with ourselves. So, we need to address what's a healthy diet for ourselves. I'm not only talking about a food diet.

Every day we feed not only our bodies, but our minds, our souls and our hearts. Some of us over indulge; some of us don't consume the right balance of foods, self-care, positive thinking, prayer/meditation, forgiveness etc. Some of us eat fast foods, some of us throw shade all day, and others just hate life, then you have those who stay in abusive relationships for no other reason than "but I love them.".

Whatever we focus on grows.

Unbeknownst to plenty of us, even small innocent habits can affect our mental and emotional health. Everything from our level of manipulation that we put up with to our use of social media can dilute mood, positivity, and sabotage our wellbeing; the relationship with ourselves.

So what can we feed ourselves to strengthen our relationship with "Self"?

I believe that a healthy relationship is not about strict limitations, having unrealistic expectations, or depriving yourself of all of the kinda-not-healthy things you love. Rather, it's about the balance and the ingredients to help the relationship with yourself run efficiently. By all means, go out, drink, smoke, have fun. But, if that's all you do, you're clearly not loving yourself, you're loving the fun only. Eventually, your demons catch up with you if you don't deal with them.

To strengthen our relationship with "Self", we need these ingredients:

Acceptance - Happiness is determined by our level of self-acceptance. It is ok to accept ourselves while still wanting better for ourselves. Self-acceptance isn't about settling for how you are today and it is not about complacency. Acceptance is about not allowing yourself to hate what you are today just because you aren't who you want to be, yet. Tomorrow isn't promised. Be happy that you made it this far. Life is a gift. Once you accept yourself, your relationship with "self" will improve.

Perspective – "A mental view, a cognitive orientation, a way of seeing a situation or a scene". My belief is that the broader our perspective, the more truth we bring into our lives, shrink our ignorance and largely enhances our inner universe. However, when we are introduced to new ideas that are foreign to us, our natural instinct is to want to reject and ignore a new viewpoint into the new ways of thinking because it is unknown or far from what we already accept as the "only way to look at it". We naturally run back to our comfort zone and shut out the new perspective if we think it's an argument of who is right vs who is wrong.

But, there are many benefits to opening our minds to varying perspectives which will then broaden our own perspective. While there is no guarantee it will change our minds, at the very least, it will keep us informed and aware of how other people see things and why they act the way they do.

Being open minded to different perspectives strengths the relationship with ourselves because it makes us more self-aware and more aware of others. It helps us accept ourselves because we realized that there is no set way to live, love, heal, grow, and succeed; there are many others ways and we can find the perspective that align with our natural lifestyles instead of conforming to perspectives that were forced upon us while growing up by society.

Commitment – commitment to personal growth helps turn desires into reality and prevents laziness and complacency. It also promotes consistency which yields trust. Enthusiasm often dissolves, but when you are committed, you'll find a way to re-spark your drive. Once you get going, momentum builds. Commitment promotes honesty and accountability. We all lie to ourselves and get too comfortable from time to time. But to beat laziness and self-deception, we have to apply pressure from commitment.

144

Dear Self,

the way you feed
yourself determines
your level of happiness.
If you do not believe
yourself to be worthy of
better love, then it does
not matter how much love
others feed you. If, on the
other hand, you do believe
yourself worthy of love, then
you will automatically give it
to yourself.

Bae Diet

When we feed our relationships with jealousy, distrust, unrealistic expectations, lies, cheating, passive aggressiveness, manipulation and resentment, it takes a toll. Over the years, I have learned what main ingredients when mixed together, improve/create healthy, happy long-lasting relationship for me.

If I feel overwhelmed by all the conflicting nutrition levels, I know that I am not alone. Most of us know the core ingredients to a relationship diet, but don't know how to manage them or work with them in such a way that'll keep both people happy.

For instance, we can't expect our communication style and level from a previous relationship to be exactly the same in the next. It's a whole new relationship and new diet, therefore we have to feed it differently.

Here is the 8 C Diet that I want to feed my next relationship: keeping our relationships healthy and exhilarating.

1. Considerate
2. Communicate
3. Compromise
4. Consistency
5. Creativity
6. Cooperate
7. Complacency (don't get stop building.)
8. Confusion (follow 1- 7 to eliminate any confusion)

Bonus - each ingredient has to be regulated differently per relationship. Communication is one thing; effective communication is another thing. Consistency is boring without creativity. There's such a thing as over compromising. And it's hard to prevent confusion.

But as long as I'm feeding my next relationship with good energy and vibes, and it's reciprocated, things could go well.

Wasted Time?

Who really wasted your time
if you are the one spending it?

Time is too valuable to be called
"wasted". We truly don't know how
much time we have. So instead of
saying it was wasted, say you just
didn't get what you expected during
a certain amount of time. But, maybe
you got something else out of it?

Always remember that it's YOUR time.
You can spend it wherever and with
whoever. You choose what you want to
do with that time.

If you are one of those people who say
"I don't have time for bullshit" truth is
you DO have time for bullshit, but just
choosing not to spend your time with
that bullshit. Nonetheless of course,
you will be spending that time with
someone or something else.

Whatever time that you feel is wasted,
you can't get that back. But you still
have control over what you do with
the remaining time that you do have.

So if you find yourself in a situation
where you feel like someone else is
wasting your time, then start spending
it somewhere else. The time is yours
and the choice is yours.

Changes

When people change,
Feelings change. That's
why I believe that when
we stay with people for
years and years, it's often
because we fall in love with
that same person over and
over again. We fall for the
little changes that people
make within themselves.
And what ends up happening
is that you either end up with
someone's changes that you
could deal with and appreciate
or you end up with someone
who has changed so much that
you don't even recognize them

Loving After Exiting

I honestly believe that it's unrealistic or unfair to say that you wouldn't date someone who still loves someone else. Some people don't have shitty break ups. We don't all hate our exes. That is why some love lives on. What changes is the desire to be together. If you take divorced couples for example; Just because they got a divorce does not mean that they do not love each other anymore. They do love each other; they just know how to accept the incompatibility, let go and fall in love with someone else.

When some people move on, they don't feel anything at all for an ex. When other people move on, they still love, just from afar. I guess I'm the type of person that loves forever. I can honestly say that I love my exes; I just don't want them. I don't feel the need to contact them or rekindle anything. I wish them the best while I'm trying to find better. I don't expect a lot of people to understand this. Just because you hate your ex doesn't mean I'll hate mine. When I see an ex, I see a person who I care about; not a woman that I want. I realize that I can love more than one person at one time when I look at my parents, my friends and family. I love all those people at the same time. Along with those people, I love some exes. I just don't desire them romantically anymore. This only makes sense to some people and that's okay. We are all different.

Love for your ex is a beautiful reminder of a happy time in your life but is also reminder of a very sad time in your life. I don't want to lose these memories because they taught me so many lessons.

In order to prove that I learned from those lessons, I choose to stay away... I don't believe we ever fully get over people we deeply love and remember. I think that we learn to live without them as the pain diminishes and wounds heal. So in order to move on, I think it's dope to remember the times we had. That's motivation for me to create better times with someone new.

No...

If you're having trouble saying no, this may help.

"Saying No Doesn't Mean You're a Bad Person"

Saying no doesn't mean that you are being rude, selfish, or petty. At a young age, we learned that saying no was viewed as impolite or inappropriate and mean. Also, saying no was off limits to adults, especially our parents. "Yes" was the respectful thing to say to adults and likable thing to say to our friends to get them to like us even if we really wanted to say "no" to everyone.

Now that we are all grown up, we are more mature and capable of making the choices that we really want to make, even if other people don't like those choices.

No, you can't have $500 dollars that you don't need, no we're not chilling and watching Netflix every night, no we're not together and not going to act like it unless we make it official. No we're not turning up every weekend. No I'm not covering your shift this time. No you can't have an extra week to pay me back. No we're not getting back together. No you can't have my number. No, no ,no no.

We live in a
generation where
we could find
a great person with
everything that
we've ever
wanted in them,
but first choose
to run away from
them or push them
away before we settle.
Because it's either too
good to be true or
too overwhelming

If you ever get
hurt again,
make sure it's
not because
you aren't
loving
yourself
enough.

Horacio Jones

We were meant
to be together,
just not meant
to last.

Horacio Jones

note to self

you can lose
yourself by
trying to find
someone else.
Don't invest
In someone
who you can
only have if
You reduce what
it means to be
yourself.

QUTOES

Equals

I believe,
Expecting to find someone
Who is my equivalent,
Is a bit unrealistic.
I want someone who
Is different.
I want someone who
I can teach things too,
And learn things from.
In a sense, I love dissimilarities.
I think the goal is to understand
The differences, and
Become the strength
to each other's
Weaknesses.

there is a big
difference between
being loved and
manipulated

cure for jealousy
if people seem to be
gaining more favorable
circumstances, going on
more vacations, buying cars,
happy in relationships, always
partying, getting promoted,
getting more "likes" and followers

.....instead of feeling down on
yourself, practice being happy for
others. It will be hard at first, but
when you cultivate true happiness
for the success of others, happiness
follows you. Try it

People cheat
when they are
afraid of love

Don't let the smile fool you.
She's still hurting, but trying
to be strong. The worst part
is that she's starting to hate
her friends because they keep
telling her what she isn't ready
to accept yet. "He Does Not Love
You." The hardest part is when
they ask "are you ok?" Because
it reminds her that she's nowhere
near "ok" and hates lying to them.
But she searches for any type of
justification for why she stays
with him.

*Sometimes you
want to take back
everything that you
feel about someone.
No matter how much
you try to paint a different
picture, at the end of the
day, some people
just don't get it.*

*I fell in love
with a part of you.
Your soul...
What I found there,
Something dark and deep.*

The reasons why you never played for keeps.

Smile

I'll admit that some days,
I miss being the reason you smiled.
But, the thing I missed the most
is smiling because of you.
I discovered peace during each smile
and I'd sit there, staring at you,
trying to read your mind even though
I loved the mystery.
For some reason,
These memories of your smile
reminded me that love
is always the right answer.
We had the choice
to hate the unknown
after breaking each other,
but instead, we chose
to let love asks questions,
and maybe it'll guide us
to its own answers
until then, I hope
you're smiling.

My Love

Your value and worth is intuitively known.
My heart needs no logic for this explanation.
I do not expect the rest of the world to understand,
and society does not validate MY love.
They cannot comprehend how your nearness
takes my breath away. In a way that the things
I want to say cannot be spoken, only showed. But,
in silence, can only hope my eyes will speak my love.
So that you can hear my heart. I don't have to prove
my love to the world. I just want to convince you
because in your mind, if we want to live happy
lives, our unique version of love is more
important than anything else.

There is a light that maybe
one day will finally show me
what it's like to be on the inside
of love.

Loving someone who
loves you back is the
ultimate compliment.

It is amazing how
everyone else can
see how evil and
sneaky someone is
while the person
emotionally involved
is oblivious to it. The
reality is, they see what's
going on, and they just
do not want to accept it.

It DOES get easier.
You will most definitely
heal and love again. However,
it won't happen overnight. These
things take time. You will notice
that with each day that goes by,
your desire to live and do things
will get stronger, and you will
think less and less about your ex
until one day you'll look back
and think, "what the hell was I
thinking, suffering so much over
that   person"

On this journey of self love,
I hope that you no longer feel
the need to search for reasons
outside of yourself just to feel
beautiful. If you need a reason
to smile, look into the mirror.
Your life is a gift.

Acceptance..... Then move the hell on. I
Challenge you to treat yourself better than
Someone else can. All along, you've been
Waiting on *"the one".*... Why not be *"the one"?*
Treating yourself better won't hurt...

The reason why she gets upset
at the people closest to her is
because she does not want anyone
to convince her to break up with
someone before she feels ready.
She knows her worth, it is just hard
to accept it for the first time. She keeps
saying that it is easier said than
done, because ending a serious
relationship is not as simple as
walking out. It is life-changing.
She'll be ready when she knows
deep down in her heart that her
relationship is going nowhere, fast.
Just try to understand how she feels and
why she is stalling. Because we've all been
there.

Do I care more
about saving
my soul than
making you
happy?

people can't read minds.

In my experience, the only way for
someone to know you have a crush on
them is for you to either tell them you
have a crush on them, or to reveal it
through your actions. People will not
simply know you have a crush on them.

She was that smile on a bad day.

And now that I do not have her,

The sun just doesn't shine

The same way.

My love cannot MAKE you worth it.

My love cannot change you.

My love cannot make you love me.

My love can only be given
unconditionally. It is up to YOU to accept
it and use your actions as proof that you
love me back.

There are two parts to a relationship.

One part comes naturally, and the

other you have to work at.

Part 1. Chemistry, magic and attraction.

Part 2. Compatibility, purpose and effort.

Chemistry is a wonderful, free spirited,

monster and it comes and goes

when it wants to.

You can't fabricate it.

To love yourself means to be in touch
with how you feel, and then acting in
a way that respects it.

Your intuition has alerted you. Trust
it before it's too late

I remove myself from people's

lives silently and gracefully.

Surround yourself with people who
aren't afraid to tell you, you're fuckin
up!!

not all men are hunters, and the
implication that women are prey
makes me uncomfortable, to be
honest.

never knew how STRONG I was until I

*had to forgive someone who wasn't
sorry*

Good men are everywhere,

but it depends on how you

look at them.

A good person to you, may be a bad
person to another and so on. BUT, even if
you find a good man, that does not mean
he will be attracted to YOU. And since he
isn't attracted to you, do you look at him
as a "bad" man all of a sudden? In
general, good guys know a lot and focus
on personal growth and inner peace
Therefore, you would have to connect at a
more open minded, healed, vulnerable
and emotional level rather than just
physical one. When you heal the parts of
you that your ex scarred, you'll start
"seeing" where the good men are.

START YOUR OWN BOOK, AND
I WILL SUPPORT YOU THROUGH
MY SOCIAL MEDIA
EMAIL ME:
HORACIOJONESJR@GMAIL.COM

Made in the USA
San Bernardino, CA
25 January 2017